At the
Chinese Table

All Under Heaven: Recipes from the 35 Cuisines of China

The Dim Sum Field Guide: A Taxonomy of Dumplings, Buns, Meats, Sweets, and Other Specialties of the Chinese Teahouse

At the
Chinese Table

A MEMOIR WITH RECIPES

Written and Illustrated by

Carolyn Phillips

W. W. NORTON & COMPANY

Independent Publishers Since 1923

Portions of this book appeared in various forms in *Vice Munchies*, *Alimentum*, *Best Food Writing 2015*, and *Life & Thyme*, as well as on the author's blog (madamehuang.com).

For information about permission to reproduce selections from this book, write to Permissions, W. W. Norton & Company, Inc., 500 Fifth Avenue, New York, NY 10110

For information about special discounts for bulk purchases, please contact W. W. Norton Special Sales at specialsales@wwnorton.com or 800-233-4830

Manufacturing by Lake Book Manufacturing
Book design by Chris Welch
Production manager: Beth Steidle

Library of Congress Cataloging-in-Publication Data

Names: Phillips, Carolyn J., author.
Title: At the Chinese table : a memoir with recipes /
written and illustrated by Carolyn Phillips.
Description: First edition. | New York : W. W. Norton & Company, [2021] |
Includes index.
Identifiers: LCCN 2021003042 | ISBN 9781324002451 (hardcover) |
ISBN 9781324002468 (epub)
Subjects: LCSH: Phillips, Carolyn J. | Food writers—United States—Biography. | Women
food writers—United States—Biography. | Cooking, Chinese. | Taiwan—
Social conditions—1975–1988. | LCGFT: Cookbooks.
Classification: LCC TX649.P49 A3 2021 | DDC 641.5951—dc23
LC record available at https://lccn.loc.gov/2021003042

W. W. Norton & Company, Inc., 500 Fifth Avenue, New York, N.Y. 10110
www.wwnorton.com

W. W. Norton & Company Ltd., 15 Carlisle Street, London W1D 3BS

1 2 3 4 5 6 7 8 9 0

To J. H. Huang and his maternal

grandmother, Liu Yukun,

for reasons that will soon become obvious

Contents

Author's Note

The recipes in this book are mainly based on food memories from my eight years in Taiwan, as well as some of the delicious meals my husband and I have enjoyed both on the Mainland and in the United States. If there is an overrepresentation of pork and garlic and sweets in here, well, you can see where my tastes lie. Please consult the Glossary and Basic Recipes beginning on page 265 for information on where to buy and how to use many of their ingredients.

A few of the ingredients called for in these recipes might prove to be difficult to find, especially if you don't live near a thriving Chinese community. You can purchase many of these staples and seasonings online, and you certainly should use every chance to stock up when you visit a good East Asian grocery store or Chinatown, but sometimes even these won't suffice. And so I've added a couple paragraphs at the end of most of the recipes to give you some ideas on how to address problems like not being able to buy winter melons and water chestnuts. As always, check out the Glossary and Basic Recipes section to find out more about these ingredients.

I have included metric measurements in addition to the usual

American cups and teaspoons and pounds. Note that with an aim toward achieving a modicum of simplicity, these usually are approximate in value (i.e., one pound in this book equals 500 grams, instead of the more accurate 454 grams), since those small increments rarely make much of a difference unless you're trying to create pastries and candy. The serving sizes for entrées take into account that these will be part of a multicourse meal unless otherwise noted.

The Pinyin form of romanization is used throughout this book, except for common place-names (such as Taipei and Kaohsiung), as well as certain names of people who are either famous or have a known preferred spelling.

A few of these experiences and conversations have been compressed or combined or retold in order to help with the flow of things, but I've done my best to provide honest recollections, as well as extrapolations based on the facts as I understand them. In any event, whatever errors you may find are mine and no one else's.

Carolyn Phillips

California, March 2020

At the
Chinese Table

Prologue

I t feels at times as if my life has been one long love affair with China. But to be honest, my desire for all that is beautiful and delicious in this ancient country really started in 1976. Back home from college that year, I was at a loss as to what to do with myself. The only thing I knew for certain was that I had a vague ambition to learn more about China—its language, its culture, its food—than my courses at the University of Hawaii had been able to offer.

My immediate problem was that even though the

Great Proletariat Cultural Revolution was beginning to wind down after thirteen long years, the doors to Mainland China seemed as if they were going to remain firmly closed for the foreseeable future to foreigners in general and Americans in particular. And then I read about a language program in Taiwan. Without giving much thought to what I was doing and why, I signed up, and within a few months found myself traveling to the other side of the world.

I naively believed that as soon as I landed in Taiwan, I would breathe in Mandarin Chinese like oxygen, that I would become fluent through some sort of magical osmosis. Surprisingly enough—to me, at least—that didn't happen. But in another way, I was incredibly lucky: Unbeknownst to me, Taipei had become, through a marvelous confluence of events, home to the foods of every region of China. The island's economy was also just beginning to take off as a consequence of the high-tech revolution, and chefs were responding to this sudden influx of money by establishing culinary shrines dedicated to any number of China's almost infinite array of unique and enchanting cuisines.

And that is why, even though I initially failed to digest much more than basic conversational Mandarin, China's gastronomy found a way to speak to me, to comfort me, to educate me, to welcome me, and to entice me into hanging in there just a little bit longer. I eventually fell in love with a scholar and gourmet who provided unexpected access into his world, and that is what, in the end, allowed me to call Taipei home for another six incredible years.

There is no doubt that he and Taiwan and the Chinese people shaped me. It is thanks to them that I ended up spending most of my adult life as a professional Mandarin interpreter before fashioning my love for the foods of China into a late-life career as a food writer and artist. Perhaps more important, though, I became part of a Chinese family whose history turned out to be intricately intertwined with that of their native land, a labyrinth of extraordinary lives.

This is my story. And theirs.

豬蹄菜酸擔湯白

Chapter 1

Unfamiliarity

TAIPEI—1976 TO 1978

T he city that sparkles below me, the one stirring itself awake window by window, hints that it is much more foreign and definitely much more exciting than I had been led to believe. In a few years, I will come to love this place more than I had ever thought possible. But right now, on this first morning in my host family's

*
5

home, I content myself with simply inhaling the sultry scents that envelop the mysterious Asian capital sprawling below me, its edges fading into the night fog and darkness.

Outside my compact little bath, the subtropical air whirls with Taipei's indefinable aroma: a heady mixture of diesel fumes, last night's rain, something or other frying, sandalwood incense, sesame oil, and the occasional gasp of cigarette smoke. Before this trip, the only foreign country I had ever managed to visit was Canada, but here I am, committed to a year on the other side of the world with only four semesters of college Chinese under my belt. As I stare out the window, I wonder whether I am being incredibly brave or abysmally foolish.

The day is September 3, 1976. I am twenty-one. Everyone I know within a three-thousand-mile radius is an acquaintance of only a few days, like me yet one more young American hoping against hope to learn Chinese. My stomach has been grumbling insistently ever since I woke up, so as soon as the sun begins to peek over the horizon, I throw on some jeans and a T-shirt, scrawl a note in Chinese that tries to suggest something on the order of "I'll be back in a couple hours," grab my house keys and a small wad of the local currency, and cram a dictionary into my back pocket. I arrange my house slippers next to the front door, put on a pair of old tennis shoes, and scurry down the apartment stairwell at high speed. I turn left as I reach the alleyway and head for the noisy thoroughfare I saw through the window, anxious to get my new life off to a tasty start.

Crossing the intersection of Songjiang and Xinyi Roads, I follow clusters of housewives and old folks slipping into tiny dark warrens between plain concrete apartment buildings, the empty shopping bags in their hands telling me everything I need to know. By the time I catch up with them, we have turned the final corner onto a wide lane, where the sounds and smells and crazy beauty of a bustling open market explode onto my senses with an almost viral intensity.

Throngs hunting down the day's supplies jostle me as I try to wriggle my way up the lane. Pyramids of brilliantly colored fruits adorn the fronts of some shops, while others are dedicated to fresh produce I don't recognize and dried ingredients I can't identify and still-flapping fish I've never before laid eyes on. Bamboo cages filled with live ducks and chickens cluster around a bench containing a chopping block and a scale, and set to the side are baskets of eggs spackled with muck and feathers. A butcher offers every part of the pig he killed during the night: precise squares of its coagulated mahogany blood submerged in clear water, and all of the animal's organs cleaned and arranged in small plastic tubs under the rows of hooks holding fresh shoulders, hams, ribs, feet, and a hairless face, as if to settle any unanswered questions as to what this animal once was.

The market smells of life and it smells of death. This is freshness on a scale I have never before encountered. I dodge the puddles from last night's squall and feel the swish of children and dogs as they careen past me through the crowds. Sometimes a person will stop, abruptly aware that I look different, and give me a stare that dissolves into a big grin. Vendors call out their wares in Taiwanese or Mandarin. Combined with the voluble discussions going on around me and the squawking of poultry, it all sounds strangely symphonic. The shoppers are bargaining for absolutely everything here, resolutely holding out for cheaper prices until money and goods change hands, and then both sides break into smiles as they wish each other a nice day.

Many of these customers snatch a bunch of
green onions or a handful of fresh chiles
as they leave, like a lagniappe or a fragrant freebie. The vendors seem to
expect this, for they have arranged
these parting favors in snagga-
ble bunches at the edges of their
stalls. It's all part of a game I
don't quite understand but am
eager to learn.

Hawkers and tiny restaurants
claim small pieces of real estate in
the market, too. My mouth salivates as I
inhale the scents of their savory rice noodles
and some sort of chowder, and I hesitate at one particularly aromatic
stand before heading on. I need something else—I don't know what,
but it will have to be really hot and really comforting. I feel logy and
hung over because my body still hasn't recovered from the exhausting flight that took me from San Jose to Los Angeles through Honolulu, and then all the way to a superlong layover in Tokyo before I was
finally released into the wilds of downtown Taipei.

My nose perks up as I turn right into a small alley. Large chunks
of meat simmer in a vat of aromatic stock by the door of a family-run
stall, and clusters of diners contentedly slurping breakfast around
the rickety tables confirm that I have come to the right place. I order
a bowl of Taiwan's famous beef noodle soup, sit down, fish a pair of
plastic chopsticks out of the rough-glazed pottery container to my
right, and lean my back against the wall. I look out over the bustling

marketplace and marvel that I have actually made it all the way to Taiwan, that I am going to have my first true Chinese meal, and that it is going to be fantastic.

THE TRUTH OF the matter is that I'm in Taipei by happenstance more than anything else. Only a few months earlier, I had come across an announcement for study abroad on a college bulletin board, had applied to both Taipei and Tokyo without giving it much thought, got accepted into the Mandarin program, and in short order found myself on my way to Taiwan. And now, with a bit of luck, maybe during my time here I'll manage to figure out what I am going to do with the rest of my life.

These initial weeks in Taiwan do turn out to be strangely wonderful because I look at my surroundings with the eyes of a child and revel in the absolute novelty of the world swirling around me. I see blurs instead of words and hear babble instead of thoughts. I hope against hope that this is temporary, for I'm starting school in less than a week. However, fast-forward a month later, and things have not improved much. Mandarin is taught using textbooks that have nothing to do with the extraordinary world outside my door, and most of my language teachers are so didactic that I feel they are almost daring me to remain mute. Even worse are my dry-as-dust classes about history, literature, and art that are taught in English by people who must have taken some sort of blood oath to keep Chinese culture firmly at an impalpable distance. After about two months of trying, I finally realize that a simple bowl of noodles is usually able

to open up a little window of comprehension that makes life here less, well, inscrutable. And that is as good an excuse as any to eat out whenever and wherever I can.

My greatest culinary discovery that first year—and an experience that led to a better understanding of modern China than any of those textbooks ever did—is a little Taipei hole-in-the-wall called Old Zhang's Dandan Noodles. This place serves little else but the classic street foods of Sichuan's capital, Chengdu. At first glance, it doesn't look like much, but a cloud of unfamiliar yet tantalizing scents puffs out the door and lures me in, so I slide warily into a seat. Because the menu proves unintelligible, I ask to be served the same thing as the guy at the next table. With rheumy growls, the waiter shouts my order out to the kitchen. Requests are met with snarls and eye contact is discouraged, giving this place all the charm and welcome of your average biker bar. But when I at last dig in, I immediately decide to dine here as often as possible. Hoping to keep this my very own secret clubhouse, I introduce it to only a tiny handful of good American friends like Leann, who will understand, who will fall in love, and who will definitely keep their mouths shut.

One day I ask a teacher why these waiters are so terrifyingly sullen, and I am told that, like most of the retired conscripts who live on the island, Old Zhang's Sichuanese waiters were once foot soldiers in Chiang Kai-shek's Nationalist Army. They had fought against either their Communist adversaries in the country's civil war or the Japanese invaders, or sometimes both. And although World War II eventually came to an end, China's civil war never really did, because instead of surrendering to Mao Zedong, Chiang and his troops decamped in 1949 to Taiwan, where they founded a separate government shored up with military backing from the United States. America's virulently anticommunist stance at the time encouraged Chiang to think that he could one day retake the Mainland, so this standoff has continued to simmer away on the back burner ever since.

But the human cost has been enormous, for family members and friends are completely cut off from one another by these implacable enemies on both sides of the Taiwan Strait. Even letters between parents and children or husbands and wives are forbidden. The hardest hit by this seem to be low-ranking military retirees, since they arrived in Taiwan alone along with their fellow conscripts and now often have to settle for jobs that barely allow them to eke by, that ensure they will never be able to support new households of their own. Thus, many of them are angrily resigned to working the rest of their solitary lives in shops where the food is familiar and the people sound like home, at places like Old Zhang's.

Typhoons scourge the island as fall takes over the calendar, as good an excuse as any to squirrel myself away in this little restaurant. At times like these, the rain pounds on the fiberglass awnings so loudly that conversation is impossible. But even if a stranger happens to sit at my table, we diligently ignore each other in order to enjoy our exquisitely spicy meals in perfect solitude. We don't even share a teapot or a word of greeting—we understand that as long as we seek refuge in this dry fortress, the other person sitting a foot away does not really exist.

As soon as my bowl is slammed on the table, I pull it forward and admire the perfectly white strands of fresh hot noodles covering the sauce so completely that this little basin gives the impression of being unadorned and innocent. And yet it is anything but. I gently toss the noodles with the hidden sauce until they are coated in a rusty glaze of ground peanuts, sesame paste, minced pork, chopped green onions and garlic, finely diced pickles, fiery chile oil, a dusting of ground toasted Sichuan peppercorns, and sweetened soy sauce. The first bite slithers across my tongue and makes me sigh, whetting my appetite for more. Soon my hunger has dulled enough for me to direct my attention to a tiny steamer basket of pork ribs skating up near my elbow. Creamier pork ribs have never existed in the annals of history: Soaked in a spicy marinade and then coated with tiny globules of steamed rice, they float over equally buttery chunks of sweet potato that have sucked up their juices and seasonings and fat. I quickly learn to squish the pork and tawny potatoes against the roof of my mouth in order to make the flavors mingle and the aromatics shoot up the back of my nose and into my sinuses. I admit, it's not an especially pretty sight, which is one more reason for me to always dine alone here.

Part of the appeal of this food definitely lies in the chiles, but they are also backed up with even more flavorings clamoring for attention: the usual aromatic trio of fresh ginger and green onions and garlic interwoven with black cardamom, salty black beans, fermented fava beans in chile paste, and the Good & Plenty reverberations of star anise, fennel, and dried licorice root. The fire of the chiles is almost always offset by what I've come to think of as the ice of Sichuan peppercorns. These tiny, pink, leathery husks numb my lips and tongue. They're more about sensory reactions than flavors, more electric than spicy, more aromatic than tasty. But, as almost always happens in the flow between Chinese and English, lingual hiccups ruin any possibility for a smooth transition. Even something as simple as these two English words—Sichuan and peppercorns—gets both salient points wrong, because what we are talking about here isn't really a variety of pepper, but rather a relative of the prickly ash. Plus, according to the most ancient of China's *materia medica*,* these plants originated somewhere farther north, around Shaanxi Province, not Sichuan. Such are the sins of inept translators.

---

* The *Shénnóng běncǎo jīng*, written about two thousand years ago.

Strange and misleading interpretations like these will compound themselves over the ensuing decades into misdirections and obfuscations that I will have to tear down before I can blindly feel my way through this colossal cultural maze. The absolute disconnect between Chinese and English will, those first few years, be my sworn enemy. In fact, I am already floundering to a stunning degree. All the classes I took in Honolulu have certainly allowed me to read better than any Chinese four-year-old, but the local preschoolers easily wipe the floor with me when it comes to saying something intelligible.

Luckily for me, I am able to say one thing right off the bat very well: *zhá páigŭ*, or fried pork chops. To my mind, this term is one of the most practical things anyone should ever know when living among the pork-loving Chinese, for it ensures, if nothing else, the possibility of a very good meal.

Few places in the world can hold a candle to the way Taiwanese chop stalls make them: Excellent-quality pork is pounded out until it is the size of a large man's hand and as thin as a china plate. This extra bit of effort by the cook at the prep end serves to break down the fibers, making the meat as silky and absorbent as a hankie. That whisper of a chop is then swished around in a thick marinade of soy sauce, garlic, and five-spice before being dredged in sweet-potato starch and deep-fried to a brittle crunch.

I sometimes wonder how much of China's gastronomic magic would have been lost if the humble pig hadn't long ago been enshrined as one of the truly lasting Han Chinese* ingredients. For all we know, a curious hominid living on the banks of North China's massive Yellow River might have been the one who discovered porky nirvana. But no matter where it all started, the first bona fide ancestors of both humans and pigs appeared during the early Pleistocene, more than two million years ago. By the Neolithic Age, which lasted from about 8000 BCE until the birth of the Bronze Age around six thousand years later, pigs were already so beloved in China that they came to decorate household items, such as the one here that shuffles its way along a bowl's surface. Somewhere around that time, the local humans came up with a written name for this delicious creature, as can be seen in the earliest Chinese character for pig, or *zhū*, which appears as a rather cute little animal balanced upright on its tail end, its head in the air and its little legs waving to the left.

* As is true with just about every other country, China is a jumble of ethnicities, but the vast majority—about 92 percent—lay claim to being ethnically Han.

Pork is still the signature ingredient in every Han Chinese cuisine—to such an extent that most mentions of meat really mean pork. Even today, dishes that the Chinese call braised meat (*shāoròu*) and shredded meat (*ròusī*) and white—or boiled—meat (*báiròu*, see page 258) invariably refer to pork, for this has always been *the* meat of China. But then again, a feast menu in *The Zhou Book of Rites* lists "eight exquisite" courses for an emperor of long ago. Starting out on a high note with roast suckling pig, it then quickly devolves into dried meat and roasted dog liver. Maybe his party tasted better than it sounds. One hopes so.

A BIG MAP OF CHINA dominates one of our classrooms and shows the borders circa 1949, back when all of Chiang's dreams went south. I have never paid it much mind, though, despite the fact that I am ostensibly here to learn Chinese and study Chinese culture, simply because Taiwan is my immediate reality, while China has faded into an abstraction. This even extends to the food, for the mother in my host family, Auntie Lee, is an extraordinary Taiwanese home cook, and every night she feeds her specialties to her family and me—like golden cabbage fritters, simple fried fish, and impossibly tender cuttlefish stir-fries.

Since Auntie Lee rarely offers much in the way of carnivore extravaganzas, whenever I'm away from home I indulge in my seemingly infinite capacity for pork, especially Taiwanese delights like little braised pork-belly sandwiches sprinkled with cilantro, peanuts, and sugar that tickle my nose and feed my appetite. Looking to create a balanced meal of sorts, I always try to buy a bag or two of whatever fruits are in season, and I have quickly come to adore the island's tiny yellow watermelons known as "little jades," the fat lychees that spurt perfumed carbonated juices over my lips and down my arms, and the "black pearl" wax apples that possess a sparkly flavor and crispy texture I cannot describe, other than to say that they are insanely good.

But the problem remains that I still don't understand the foods of all the other provinces and culinary capitals of China. I'll traipse my way down Yongkang Street, say, to eat a chicken braised with a mountain of mysterious spices, and although the sign announces that this dish originated in Henan, I haven't a clue as to where that province is or why it matters or what role it played in Chinese history. I read the words *Shanxi* or *Chaozhou* on other menus, and all they tell me at this point is whether I'll be served something made of wheat or rice.

And so it goes, until a bowl of extravagantly seasoned Xi'an-style hand-pulled noodles piques my curiosity enough to make me take a more careful look at that vast map. Then I remember having read that emperors had long ago sited their capital there as a defensive garrison, albeit with the most enviable of palaces and the greatest of dining pleasures hidden within its ramparts. The imperial headquarters once called Chang'an* lies far to the southwest of Beijing, and so, still wondering why its foods have such striking aromatics, I run my finger along a dotted line tracing the path of the ancient

---

* Chang'an ("Lasting Peace") is today renowned as Xi'an ("Western Peace"), the home of Qin Shihuang's terracotta army.

Silk Roads that once linked the Middle East and Central Asia with China, out in the vast windswept lands where the Great Wall crumbles into the sand dunes. A vision of caravans laden with heavy loads of fragrant spices traveling east along the Imperial Highway makes the multilayered flavors in that bowl of noodles come alive.

I store that tidbit of information in my mental Rolodex for later on, when I have more details to work with. But until then, with food supplying all sorts of clues, these place names cease to be mere notions, and I take closer and longer looks at that big old map as I consider what I'm going to have for lunch.

DECONSTRUCTING THE LAYOUT of China was difficult, but food showed me the way, for I happened to be in the very right place for just the right handful of years. Once upon a time and over a couple of delectable decades, Taiwan was home to the greatest assemblage of Chinese cuisines in the world, and it all started in 1949.

Only four years after the end of World War II and all the atrocities that China had suffered at the hands of the Japanese, the Nationalists were losing in their civil war with the Communists. Chiang Kai-shek led his troops to a last, fortified stand on China's smallest province, the island of Taiwan. Fortunately for all concerned, many of the country's most inspired chefs had packed up and accompanied waves of wealthy and well-connected Mainlanders as they crossed the Taiwan Strait. Family cooks, talented soldiers with a longing for the foods of their ancestral villages, and gastronomes of every stripe and from every province filled in all the gaps. The sum of China's widely diverse cuisines was suddenly in one place. The thing is, though, as with so many complex food cultures like India and Mexico, the most creative culinary minds in China were much more likely to work in private homes than in restaurants.

Even nowadays, public restaurants are not where the rich and famous prefer to eat, despite the fact that China's people have been dining out for at least a thousand years—as can be seen in the massive scroll painting *Along the River During the Qingming Festival*—for China's culinary arts were more often than not developed in royal palaces, for the tables

---

* Part of the Palace Museum's collection in Beijing, this long handscroll was painted by Zhang Zeduan during the Northern Song dynasty (960–1127) and is one of the nation's most famous and prized landscapes. *Qīngmíng shànghé tú* depicts a number of men enjoying themselves at eating establishments in the city we now know as Kaifeng in Henan Province. Perhaps even more important, this painting proves that the first restaurants weren't invented in postrevolutionary France to feed the proletariat. Rather, dining establishments of all sorts were already quite commonplace in China at a time when Europe was just beginning to crawl its way out of the Dark Ages.

of the well-to-do, and with the enjoyment of the literati in mind. This is described beautifully in one of the country's most renowned cookbooks, *The Sui Garden Gastronomy* (*Suíyuán shídān*),* which contains 326 recipes for dishes the poet Yuan Mei enjoyed in the dining rooms of friends and fellow gourmets during the late 1700s, not to mention the creations of his own kitchen, rather than in commercial establishments. And that tradition has continued to this day.

---

* Yuan Mei's abode, or *Suíyuán*, is variously rendered in English as the "Garden of Contentment" or the "Garden of Accommodation" or the "Harmony Garden." The reason why its English equivalent is so hard to pin down is because, as Master Yuan himself pointed out, the former owner of his lands in Jiangsu's capital of Nanjing had been surnamed Sui, and so—showing the proper humility of a learned man—he only went so far in renaming it as to use a homonym that basically means *to follow* or *to comply with*, which, of course, doesn't exactly flow off the tongue in English.

It should be pointed out that Master Yuan is beloved not only because he wrote one of China's classic cookbooks, but also because he was a forerunner in promoting the education of women, a patron of the arts who eventually surrounded himself with so many talented poetesses that he collected their work under the title of his garden.

Another reason why Taipei's greatest dining destinations didn't exist until a quarter century or so after these chefs arrived was due to its less than robust economy, as well as the civil war between Taiwan and the Mainland that had providentially settled down into volleys of words, rather than bullets. Chiang's death in 1975 (and Mao's in 1976) gave the island's government a very timely excuse to loosen its grip on society just enough so that Taiwan could latch onto the same high-tech revolution that was revving up near my mom's home in Silicon Valley. Even more important to my story is that not long after that, those suddenly wealthy and also very hungry entrepreneurs began convincing many brilliant private chefs to open culinary palaces in downtown Taipei.

In short, Taiwan's capital was in the midst of transforming itself into a food-lover's paradise at just the moment I appeared on the scene, and I have to admit that I took full advantage of the situation.

ALMOST EVERY AMERICAN I know of has left for more familiar territory by the end of their second year, if not before. The reason given (usually accompanied with a deep sigh) is that living any longer as a foreigner in Taipei is just too exhausting. Finding myself now trapped in the strange existence afforded to second-year language students, I am beginning to understand why.

Part of the problem is that I live alone in an apartment near the upper edge of town, so I no longer can rely on a handy American environment to swallow me up. Instead, I have what I thought I had wanted: total immersion. However, I remain unable to speak well enough to fit into society out here in the Songshan District. I also know for a certainty that I will never come close to mimicking the way the people here move and dress. I react to this by turning even more thin-skinned and irritable, for I have a sneaking feeling that my presence is always being commented upon, laughed at, mocked. I have been doubling down on my ninja act, too. Umbrellas are popped open to shield me from stares, as much as from the sun and the rain. I don massive sunglasses à la Jackie Onassis. I wind my chestnut hair into a tight knot at my nape and shove it under a hat or scarf, the better to conceal its attention-getting color. I cover my mouth when I laugh. I wear skirts and pumps. I strive to be a worker bee in this massive hive. Every day I have to navigate endless cultural landmines in those high heels, and I am clumsily tripping over them to an alarming degree.

Despite the undeniable lure that returning to the States poses to me on a daily basis, I'm still not yet ready to capitulate. My mother and I talk once a month, and she generally winds up the call with some variation on the theme of *When are you coming back?* And I counter with *Later,* and *Give me time.* I want to learn this language and somehow, someday fit in, but the problem is that I wrestle Chinese into my brain only long enough to take a test before it slithers right back out again.

But even if I did decide to give up, I have nowhere to go and no money to do it with. Mom and I, well, we tried our best, but the only time we ever spent enjoying each other's company was when we traveled around Taiwan, Hong Kong, and Japan at the end of my first year here. Because she was linguistically at my mercy for four weeks, our power dynamic was upended. We became equals of sorts, and for some strange reason this freed her up in ways I hadn't thought possible. I never saw her so alive or laugh so much. But by then it was too late—she and I had grown too far apart, for I was turning into someone else on the other side of the world. Mom said ruefully, again and again in those long-distance calls, that I wasn't her little girl anymore, that she didn't recognize me. And, as for me, I am painfully aware that I can never go back to her way of life.

Which means that I'm trapped in a place that makes no sense and I have no way out. It's like one of those fairy tales where the trees close behind me after each step and only a murky path forward shows itself. I feel my way along the dirt, stum-

bling over rocks. I am now so deep in the forest that even starlight cannot guide my feet. If I stop, a branch creeps up and nudges me onward. I almost hope that a witch's hut is around the bend, because frankly I could kill for some ginger-bread, or, even better, a little conversation in English with some wizened crone before she tried to stuff me into her oven.

At least I'd know what was going on.

Taiwanese Fried Pork Chops

TÁISHÌ ZHÁ PÁIGǓ 台式炸排骨

Memorize this recipe. It will become beloved.

MARINADE

    2 cloves garlic, finely minced

    3 tablespoons mild rice wine

    1 tablespoon regular Chinese soy sauce

    1 teaspoon five-spice powder

    ¼ teaspoon cayenne (optional)

    Freshly ground black pepper

THE REST

    2 boneless pork chops (about 12 ounces | 350 g total)

    1 cup | 140 g sweet-potato starch

    Oil for frying

    Sea salt, as needed

First, prepare the marinade by mixing together the garlic, rice wine, soy sauce, five-spice, optional cayenne, and black pepper to taste in a medium bowl. Set aside.

Pat the chops dry with a paper towel. The chops should be no more than ½ inch | 1 cm thick at this point, so slice heftier cuts in half horizontally. Lay one chop on your board and use the flat back of a heavy knife (*not the blade*) to whack up and down the chop so that the entire surface becomes tightly ridged. Turn the chop 90 degrees and whack up and down again, and really work on any streaks of fat, as that is where the tendons hide. Turn the chop over and whack the other side. When you are finished, the chop should be thin (no more than ¼ inch | 6 mm thick) and look almost fluffy, but not falling apart. Repeat this step with the other chop or chops. Flip the chops around in the marinade to coat both sides. Cover the bowl and refrigerate for at least 20 minutes, and up to a couple of hours.

Pour the starch into a wide bowl and set a large plate or baking sheet next to it. Dip one of the chops in the starch, carefully coating it completely, then gently shake off any excess and set the chop on the prepared plate or pan. Repeat with the other chop.

Pour about 1 inch | 2 cm of oil into a wok and heat over medium-high heat. When the tip of a wooden or bamboo chopstick inserted in the hot oil is immediately covered with bubbles, slide one of the chops into the oil so that it lies flat, cover the wok with a spatter guard, and fry the pork, turning once, until it is golden brown and crispy on both sides. Remove the chop to a clean cutting board and repeat with the other chop. When the pork is cool enough to handle, cut it crosswise into strips and sprinkle lightly with salt. Serve with hot steamed rice and whatever condiments sound good to you. The Garlic Chile Sauce on page 147 is a delectable accompaniment. *Serves 2 as an entrée, 4 as part of a multicourse meal.*

Tip

Sweet-potato starch is classic here and will always give you the best results, period. It's available online, so try to hunt it down. Cornstarch will do if you must have fried pork chops and cannot wait—be assured that I fully understand and approve. Tapioca starch is a third option, but since it has a tendency to turn gummy whenever it goes on too thickly, proceed accordingly.

Golden Cabbage Fritters (V)

ZHÁ GĀOLÌCAÌ WÁN 炸高麗菜丸

This homey Taiwanese classic is simplicity itself, for it's just shredded vegetables bound with starch and eggs before being fried into crispy little nuggets. The mom in my host family served this dish often, yet I never got tired of it. As with all her other creations, she didn't ever consult a recipe or cookbook but rather relied on memories of years spent in the kitchen. Unlike most other versions I've tried, hers was all about the vegetables, and the batter is there only to keep things stuck together, making it almost tempura-like with its ethereal texture.

DIPPING SAUCE

¼ cup | 60 ml Garlic Chile Sauce (page 147)

2 tablespoons balsamic or rice vinegar

Sugar to taste

FRITTERS

¼ head cabbage (about 8 ounces | 225 g), finely shredded into
   pieces no longer than 1 inch | 2 cm

½ medium carrot, peeled and grated

¼ medium yellow or red onion, finely shredded

3 large eggs, lightly beaten

3 tablespoons cornstarch

2 tablespoons all-purpose flour

1 teaspoon baking powder

½ teaspoon fine sea salt

Oil for frying

First, make the sauce by stirring the chile sauce with the vinegar and sugar. Let it mellow while you prepare the fritters.

Place the cabbage, carrots, and onion in a medium bowl. Mix in the eggs, then sprinkle in the cornstarch, flour, baking powder, and fine sea salt, and mix all together.

Preheat the oven to 250°F | 120°C. Place a piece of parchment paper on a heatproof platter.

Pour about ½ inch | 1 cm of oil into a large frying pan and heat over medium-high heat until hot but not smoking. Working in batches, use chopsticks to pick up the batter-covered vegetables and transfer them to the hot oil. Don't overcrowd these little haystacks, as you want to have enough room for them to flutter around the surface and not stick together. Fry them on both sides until done, then remove to the platter and keep hot in the oven. Serve hot, with the dipping sauce. *Serves 4.*

Tips

If fresh Fresno chiles cannot be found for love or money in your area, spring for a bottled Chinese chile sauce (Lee Kum Kee has some good ones), or use whatever sauce you'd like.

Your mileage may vary on how much water the vegetables dump out into the batter. Therefore, just before you fry the haystacks, if everything looks a bit runny, drain out the extra liquid and you'll be good to go.

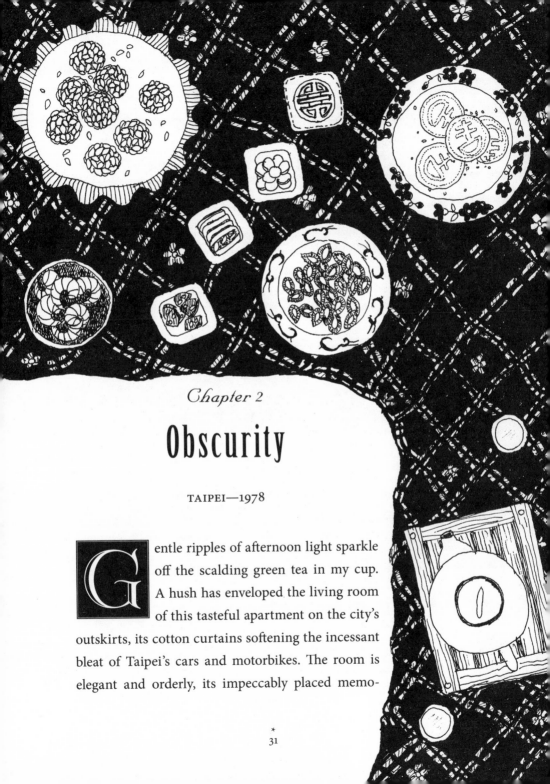

Chapter 2

Obscurity

TAIPEI—1978

Gentle ripples of afternoon light sparkle off the scalding green tea in my cup. A hush has enveloped the living room of this tasteful apartment on the city's outskirts, its cotton curtains softening the incessant bleat of Taipei's cars and motorbikes. The room is elegant and orderly, its impeccably placed memorabilia testifying to an organized mind and a life well lived. All of this would be the perfect recipe for relaxation for anybody else, but the unaccustomed silence is pinging against my nerves. Looking for something to do, I touch my tiny eggshell teacup and feel my fingertips practically weld to its blistering surface, so I go back to sitting motionless and upright, as is expected of me.

Professor Gao Zi gracefully floats across the parquet floor with a vessel full of hot water to top off her fist-size teapot. She asks in Mandarin, "How do you like the tea?" I murmur something appreciative about the aroma and dearly hope I am getting all the Chinese tones

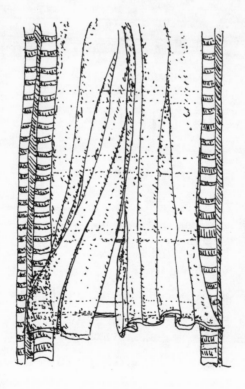

right. She chuckles softly and returns to her tiny kitchen. I get up to follow this legendary teacher of dance, her thin frame barely rustling her gray traditional dress, but she waves me back into my chair. Sepia photos on her end tables, framed calligraphy flowing down foxed paper, and worn volumes on the shelves speak of a scholar's den, while a small vase of flowers lightens up a corner and adds a feminine touch. Every other room on this subtropical island carries at least a faint undercurrent of mildew and damp, but nature has been firmly tamed in my hostess's home, so my nose twitches pleasurably at the bouquet of Chinese ink, tung oil on the furniture, brewing tea, and the sweet tobacco scent of browned old books.

It is 1978, a day in late summer. I am the sole guest at the home of a spirited feminist and scholar as old as the century. And there I sit, less than a third her age, an American observer with a deep feeling of unease over how little I understand the world around me. I'm here mainly because I have been reading about the women's rights movement in China during the early twentieth century, and I'm trying to make myself excited about this as a possible theme for a master's thesis. I've been buying a small library of Chinese materials on the subject, as well as memoirs and collections of newspaper articles from the 1920s. The last step in this project consists of hunting down people to interview who had actually lived through that part of history. They're getting on in years, and I will have to hurry if I am going to make it work.

The first one to take me up on this is Professor Gao. I know my interview will be a struggle for both of us, as she speaks very little English. So, while she sets out things for us to nibble on, I rehearse my questions in my head and hope desperately that I'll make a good impression.

As she disappears once again into her kitchen, my mind does what it does best nowadays: spins its wheels. Part of the reason for my inability to concentrate is that I am always hungry and dizzy, for, to put it bluntly, my guts are in serious rebellion. Everybody says with authority that this is to be expected with any newcomer—and I'm definitely still considered one, even after two years—for *shuǐ tǔ bùfú*: the water and soil are proving incompatible with this body of mine. It's gotten to the point where I'm losing weight so fast that I have to rely on sturdy diaper pins to keep my skirts and pants up.

In this weakened state, rude jolts batter my cosseted little brain whenever I let down my protective shields. These easily range from the inane to the horrifying and then back to the inane again over the course of a day. At the low end of the scale, for example, is the fact that few people ever try to match up their outfits here, so plaids and paisleys, stripes and argyles are mixed together in a rainbow of colors that is not half as delightful as the word *rainbow* suggests. Censors whack much of the violence and sex out of foreign movies before I get to see them, including what might very well include the pivotal scenes, so I sometimes leave a movie like *Taxi Driver* or *Carrie* absolutely bewildered. Nevertheless, Hollywood thrives here. All over the city, big billboards advertise chestnuts like the 1940 remake of *Waterloo Bridge*, starring Robert Taylor and Vivien Leigh, as well as relatively current films. These are painted by hand to provide room for the Chinese versions of the titles and stars' names. Striving for authenticity—for women here don't yet shave—the painters inevitably insert color-appropriate armpit hair on the glamorous females posing for, say, *Shampoo* and *The Man with the Golden Gun*, although I seriously doubt that would have made either Julie Christie or Britt Ekland very happy.

And then I run across things that haunt my nightmares. Too many limping feral dogs are so covered with mange that they look more like lepers than canines. Too many young people are crippled by polio, and too many girls are for sale in the red-light districts. Too many beggars with missing body parts lay claim to the underpasses alongside too many raggedy children. And I now know the Chinese words for *goiter* and *hunchback* and *taxi dancer*—not that I really want to.

Spend enough time with these horrors and even everyday life will get under your skin. You no longer notice the things that bring us together as humans, but rather all the little discrepancies that set our societies apart: The tap water has to be boiled ten minutes before it is potable. Ice is never an option outside your home or a big hotel because you don't know the source of the water. Root vegetables and lettuce are not served raw because night soil—human feces—fertilizes the farms. Open sewers line the streets under heavy gutter grates, and the stench during the hot months is almost visible. I tell myself that all this is simply culture shock, and not everyone is going to be particularly excited about accommodating my tender sensibilities, but now even the toilet paper annoys me to no end, for it comes in large squares that nest in a box atop the toilet tank.

Most of the problems Taiwan faces at this time can be safely laid at the feet of Chiang Kai-shek. His rise to power on the Mainland was supported by the notorious Green Gang of Shanghai back when that East China city was the vice capital of the world. Chiang eventually adopted fascist tendencies to such an extent that he had himself referred to as *generalissimo*, and he even ended up looking like an Asian version of Spain's Francisco Franco—down to the cape, mustache, medals, and khaki uniform. But sartorial achievements aside, Chiang didn't accomplish much, and he certainly did not put a whole lot of effort into improving the lives of his people. He probably would have thought that a waste of time, for although Chiang maintained an iron grip on Taiwan between 1949 and 1975, he pictured himself as a leader in exile, and all his hopes were pinned on somehow retaking the Mainland. He died the year before I showed up without having made any headway on that score, and the society that surrounds me is still wrestling with his shadow, as well as curfews, draconian drug laws, one-party rule, flourishing prostitution and organized crime, and a censored press. Peking opera music screeches out from the television set on designated days because that's what our very own generalissimo liked. Nobody seems to notice or care that the programming and the laws can be safely changed now that he is dead.

I SLAP ON a smile and stand up when the clinking of porcelain containers on a wooden tray announces the return of my hostess. Arrayed on the low table between us are small china dishes holding more dried and candied tea snacks than we could possibly consume in one sitting.

Little saucers and bowls are arranged deftly on the polished wood, and I watch with rapt attention as her aged hands take apart the stack of blue and white porcelain, each compartment revealing a few edible gems much like a jewelry box. These doll-size containers hold dry coins of sliced ruby hawthorn paste, pine nuts frozen in golden pyramids of caramelized sugar like ants in amber, pale ribbons of rice flour bordering slender dominoes of toasted walnuts and ground black sesame, moss-colored cakes of mung bean flour stamped with auspicious symbols and filled with red bean paste, bite-size cookies smothered with toasted sesame seeds, dried watermelon seeds salted and subtly flavored with star anise, and delicate tan cubes of peanut and sesame brittle.

"*Shìyīxià zhèxiē*," Professor Gao invites me, directing my attention to the mung bean cakes. I gingerly pick one up, hoping that it won't collapse halfway between the plate and my mouth. Nibbling off a fragment, I enjoy the toasted aroma of the sesame oil and the hint of salt tingling against the sweetness of the red bean paste within. The morsel dissolves into soft wet sand once it hits my tongue and then vanishes. A tentative sip of my tea tastes slightly astringent at first, but then it turns sweet when it washes across my tongue.

My hostess and I exchange pleasantries while we sidle up to my discussion with her. If I had been honest that day—as much to myself as to her—I would have confessed that my language skills were really not up to the task and I was just wasting her time. But instead, I keep up these pretenses, filling the spaces in our conversation with more or less appropriate words. While we talk about her life, she invites me to try one of the lumps of amber poised on her table. I bite down hard on an edge, and it sends shards of candy and crumbly pine nuts onto my tongue. Savoring how the caramel's bitter edge softens the sweetness, I push the tiny bits of sugar and nuts around my teeth until they dissolve.

Hers is a dainty feast of almost fairylike perfection. I have never before been a solitary guest at an older Chinese person's house, and it occurs to me as I graze my way across the table that I am way out of my element, for these snacks were designed back in old Suzhou to perfectly complement a fine pot of tea, preferably in some summery pavilion idyllically perched inside a languid lotus pond.

My eyes alight on a celadon saucer at the edge of my hostess's generous array of tea snacks. Six dried shrimp the size of quarters are piled there in an acrobatic tumble. They look too perfect to be real, as if someone with a fanatical attention to detail had carved them out of coral. My hostess nudges them toward me. I waver a half-second too long, so she picks up one and takes a tiny bite, silently suggesting that I do likewise. Gingerly plucking a shrimp by its tail, I thread an edge through my lips and guillotine off a shard. The sea resounds on my palate as microscopically thin flakes of salt come loose, crash on my taste buds, and waft up through my nose. I start to chew, and the funky flavors of its flesh mingle with the brackish flavors of the sea. A sip of the same bitter green tea now suggests something floral on the edge, a transformation that confuses me. As I work the crustacean around in my mouth, I find that this really is nothing more than your basic dried shrimp, with no fancy coating to counter the brininess and no sesame seeds to distract. It is startling in its natural simplicity, singularly brave and confident, and in marked contrast to the stunning—yet ineffably manmade—sweet tidbits that decorate her table.

Pouring some more tea into my hostess's cup before refilling my own, I take a cautious sip and notice that, thanks to the dried shrimp, a scent of honey combined with plum blossoms has now supplanted the last echoes of green. I thoughtfully chew on the rest of the shrimp and revel in the way my nose and tongue are reacting to these unusual sensations. Pretty soon I'm paying more attention to what is happening inside my delicate white teacup, too, as the tea cycles through a series of colors—pale straw, caterpillar green, deep olive, buttery yellow—and its own progression of aromas, with shades of perfume, bitterness, and summer sun gracing each thimble of the ever-changing brew. Every tenth cup or so, Professor Gao ceremoniously replaces the raggedy used leaves in her brick-hued Yixing pot with fresh needles of Dragon Well tea. Using an aged bamboo scoop no

wider than my thumb, she delicately measures them out of a metal canister so old and beloved that much of its paint has worn off. As I watch her, I realize with immense gratitude that, instead of setting out a simple tea party, she has allowed me to participate in a meditation on flavors and aromas and spectrums I previously hadn't even known existed.

Grazing my way for another hour through endless cups and that parade of edible jewels, I listen to the wonderful cadences in my hostess's voice as everything on her table speaks to me and demands that I acknowledge how extraordinarily perfect they really are. And while they do that, various puzzle pieces start to drift into place. I suddenly grasp with deep delight that the problem all along has been with my approach, not with this land and its people. The anxiety that has twisted my insides for so long relaxes its hold. My stomach begins to rumble. By the end of our tea, I find myself absolutely ravenous, even though I did little but nibble all afternoon. And so, once I say my good-byes and slip around the corner, I duck into an aromatic little snack shop in order to devour an enormous bowl of hot sesame noodles. A welcome warmth surges through me.

Forcing myself to eat out alone in the ensuing months while surrounded by Chinese diners, I blindly order whatever I see in front of them, and a new learning process begins. I hunt for tiny holes-in-the-wall that serve dishes I've never heard of, and I ask every Chinese person I know where I should eat, and what, and why. I develop an addiction to things like deep-fried stinky doufu (a.k.a. tofu or bean curd) slathered with crisp fermented cabbage and doused in smoky chile oil. I'm told that I begin to smile more, and those diaper pins that once held my clothes together are tossed out as my body recovers some of its lost upholstery.

I continue to scale that sheer wall inch by inch throughout my last few months of living alone in Taiwan. Of course, many more plateaus and dead ends will have to be negotiated along the way. But as far as I'm concerned, the key to understanding China can be found in learning to appreciate the foods from a Chinese point of view, a task that is every bit as pleasant—and every bit as daunting—as it sounds.

Perched on the edge of an ancient civilization, on the outside looking in, I have at last found myself standing on top of the wall. Now all I have to do is follow my nose.

And over that wall I go.

Chinatown-Style Almond Cookies (V)

TÁNGRÉNJIĒ XÌNGRÉN BǏNGGĀN 唐人街杏仁餅乾

I will never be able to re-create all the exquisite teatime snacks that Professor Gao set before me, but I do love a good cookie. In fact, I have adored the crumbly almond cookies made in San Francisco's Chinatown ever since I was a little girl. My mother, maternal grandmother, and I once took the train from San Jose up to San Francisco. Because this was a really big deal for us, we all donned hats and gloves. We then wandered around Chinatown, and in addition to begging for a big pink box of these cookies, I also managed to wheedle my mother and grandmother into getting me bags of candied coconut, dried lychees, and sugar-coated almonds. No wonder I headed off to Taipei fifteen years later.

COOKIES

> ¾ cup | 145 g organic solid vegetable shortening, good lard, or unsalted butter
>
> ½ cup | 100 g granulated sugar
>
> ¼ cup | 45 g coconut sugar or packed dark brown sugar
>
> 1 large egg
>
> 1 tablespoon almond extract
>
> 2 teaspoons vanilla extract
>
> ¾ cup | 100 g ground almonds

1¾ cups | 165 g unbleached pastry flour

¾ teaspoon fine sea salt

¾ teaspoon baking soda

TOPPING

1 large egg, lightly beaten

32 whole almonds, unblanched or blanched (with or without
skin)

Place the shortening or lard, both sugars, the egg, and both extracts
in the bowl of a food processor. Whiz them for around a minute,
stopping the machine now and then to scrape down the sides, until
you have a very light, creamy mixture. Mix together the ground
almonds, pastry flour, fine sea salt, and baking soda in a small bowl.
Add this mixture to the food processor and pulse until the dough is
evenly mixed.

Lay 2 sheets of parchment paper or foil on your work surface.
Scrape half of the dough onto each sheet, spread each portion into
an even, 8-inch | 20-cm long log-like shape, and roll the dough up in
the paper or foil like a cigar. Freeze the dough for about 20 minutes,
just until it is solid but still easy to cut.

Place the racks in the upper and lower thirds of your oven and set
it to 275°F | 135°C. Line two baking sheets with Silpats or parchment
paper.

Cut each log of dough into 16 even pieces. (The dough may feel
slightly sticky at this point, but that's normal.) Place them on the
lined sheets about 2 inches | 5 cm apart. Brush each slice with beaten
egg and then press a whole almond in the center.

Bake the cookies for 25 minutes. Rotate the sheets from top to bottom and back to front, and increase the heat to 325°F | 160°C. Continue to bake for about 10 minutes more, until the cookies are golden brown. Remove from the oven and let cool to room temperature on the sheets. Store them in an airtight container at room temperature or freeze for longer storage. *Makes 32 cookies.*

Crunchy Breakfast Rice Rolls (V)

ZĪFÀNTUÁN 粢飯糰

The sweet version of these rice rolls was without a doubt my preferred breakfast during my first few months in Taipei because a nice middle-aged Taiwanese lady would plant herself in front of my language school every weekday morning and sell them from her simple cart. No wonder I was so besotted with them, for they are the perfect diet combination of hot sticky rice, fried dough, toasted peanuts, and sugar.

> Half a fried Chinese cruller (*see* Tip, as well as Glossary and
>   Basic Recipes)
> About 4 cups | 700 g freshly cooked sticky rice
> ½ cup | 65 g chopped toasted peanuts
> ½ cup | 70 g toasted sesame seeds
> ½ cup | 100 g sugar, or to taste

Heat the oven to 300°F | 150°C. Split the cruller down the middle into 2 long strips and then cut each strip into 2 equal pieces. Place them on a small baking sheet and heat in the oven until very crispy. (If you prefer, you can bake these at 275°F | 135°C for a longer time, until they are hard.)

If the rice is still super-hot, first lay a clean, dry washcloth on your counter, then cover it with a large clean resealable plastic bag and top this with a 12-inch- | 30-cm-wide piece of plastic wrap. The washcloth will protect your hands, the plastic bag will give you a nice slippery surface, and the plastic wrap will keep the sticky rice manageable; if the rice is cool enough to handle, you can omit the washcloth.

Scoop a quarter of the hot rice onto the middle of the plastic wrap and use a silicone spatula to spread it out into a more or less 8-inch | 20-cm square. Sprinkle a quarter of the peanuts, sesame seeds, and sugar down the middle and lay a piece of toasted cruller on top. Use all three (or two, if you aren't using the washcloth) layers of the wrapping to roll up the rice and condiments around the cruller, patting the ends in as you go to seal in everything. Lightly squeeze the rice roll in your hands to compact it and keep it from falling apart. If necessary, reposition the plastic wrap around the rice roll, and serve it still wrapped, so that the diner can peel back the wrap after each bite. Repeat to make a total of 4 rolls. *Makes 4 rice rolls.*

Tip
Frozen Chinese crullers (long, soft doughnut strips with no sugar or toppings on them) will most likely only be available in a Chinese grocery or Cantonese deli. That means that you might have to get creative here. Mexican *churros* (which are a bit similar, as these are long, crunchy doughnut strips dredged in cinnamon sugar) will work in a pinch if you knock most of the coating off (or keep it on if you want to enjoy cinnamon rice rolls—I'm not judging), or you could even fry up some wonton skin strips. What you want is something crunchy and fairly bland to offer contrast. The results will still be sensational no matter what you do.

Chapter 3

Avidity

SOUTHERN TAIWAN AND TAIPEI—1978

He loads me up on a train one morning with promises of adventure and good food. I protest that we don't have the money to waste on first-class seats, but this boyfriend of mine brushes my objections aside with barely restrained glee as he describes the seafood of southern Taiwan, its aromatic fruits,

its delicious night markets. The porter hands me a boxed lunch somewhere south of the newly booming high-tech city of Hsinchu, and I sullenly poke my chopsticks at the cold rice and flavorless pork chop, vastly unimpressed so far with this trip of his down memory lane.

My mood softens as the buildings outside the train window disappear into an endless checkerboard of glassine rice paddies mirroring the hot sun. Our car bumps and sways too much for photographs, so I just wave to the farmers as we trundle past at slow speed. Alongside them, ankle-deep in the mud, are women so swathed against the harsh sunshine in their colorful cotton wraps and conical hats that only their eyes remain visible, but their waves seem to welcome us to Taiwan's tropical farmlands.

The boyfriend's head nods lower and lower until it drops onto my shoulder, the combination of a full stomach and the gentle rocking of the train finally proving irresistible. I gradually push J. H.* barely upright and remove a sketchbook from my bag. I outline his face with a freshly sharpened No. 2 pencil and then redraw his chin a few times until it looks like him. Having the man asleep next to me

---

* His Chinese name in Pinyin is Huang Zhuhua. His given name means "Pillar of China" and was romanized as *Juh-hwa* somewhere along the way. He long ago gave up on getting any non-Chinese to pronounce his name correctly, so he just uses initials. I tried to convince him many times to use the name James instead, so that he could introduce himself as, "Huang, James Huang," but he failed to find the humor in that. His parents likewise had their names rendered into English as Lung-chin Huang and Yueh-ming Chou, but I've gone with their Pinyin spellings here, since they so rarely used those hyphenated versions.

gives me the rare chance to stare at him, pencil in hand, and figure out all the little curves in his nose and mouth that make him unique. He moved in only about two months ago, so his face still looks like a stranger's at times, but as I draw him over and over, his features come into sharper focus and turn more familiar. My fingertips can almost feel the roundness of his eyes under their lids as I sketch them, the tear-shaped dimple astride his lip, the slope and dip above his nose. He mumbles something and angles his face toward the roof of the car. I flip the page and start a new portrait, my fingers finally understanding how to re-create the little loop on the inside of each eye. I switch to a harder pencil and flick in the fine black hairs of his lashes and eyebrows.

We travel all day by train and arrive somewhere around late afternoon in the massive port city of Kaohsiung. The next morning, we catch a bus to Donggang, or "East Harbor," for his family used to live in a military compound on its northern outskirts. Once a laidback fishing community, the village by now has grown up. J. H. and I wander around as he tries to remember where things used to be. We follow the signs to a few local sites, like the elaborately decorated Donglong Temple dedicated to such Daoist deities as the ones who protect fishermen, but otherwise we are lost until we find our way to the fish markets. Most of the wooden boats docked here are multicolored scows—little more than basic cabins astride

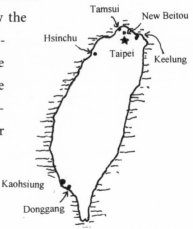

flat-bottomed vessels—with a large eye painted on either side of the prow to protect the fishermen by keeping watch on the endless waves.

We are ravenously hungry by the time we check out the dining stalls along Dapeng Bay, and as we try to decide among them, one of the cooks says my boyfriend looks vaguely familiar and draws him into a conversation. This is J. H.'s first time back in almost a decade, so he enthusiastically reports that his mom taught Chinese in the local high school. The cook remembers her as one of his favorite teachers and remarks on how much he looks like his mother. He invites us to sit down for a meal, and almost immediately the food starts to arrive, both the things we ordered and all the cook's little treats. The first is a platter of quickly steamed live prawns, sweet and juicy, with a garlicky dipping sauce on the side to whet our appetites. A couple of crabs are chopped up and stir-fried with green onions and cloudlike scrambled eggs. The bodies of fat cuttlefish are crosshatched into fine feathers before a quick tour in the wok barely cooks them through, and they are so lusciously tender that they disappear before I can remember eating them. Sun-moon scallops—so named because they are large, flat, and round, with one side white and the other a deep maroon—are steamed and served with a puckery sauce that makes their rich flavor pop. Dish after dish arrives, until we are almost exhausted from eating so much and so well. A clear soup of tiny shelled oysters and ginger threads concludes the meal. It is without a doubt the most extraordinary meal I've eaten to date.

After a postprandial chat with the owner about life in the village and the high school, we wander off in search of the station so we can catch a late train back to Kaohsiung. But it's nowhere to be found. As the sun settles behind the tall betel palms that line the town, an elderly resident sitting on a park bench advises us that the old feeder line no longer exists, which means that we will have to stay in Donggang overnight. We look at each other, shrug, and ask to be pointed to a hotel.

Night has arrived when we are finally shown our room in a local flophouse. Crimson splashes cover its walls and floors, and all I can smell in the humid tropical air is effluvia caked with sweet anise. J. H. assures me that what I'm seeing isn't actually blood, but rather betel nut juice,* for

---

* Betel nuts, or *bīnláng,* are popular throughout the world. They are a cheap, readily available narcotic that helps regular joes like taxi drivers and farmers get through the day. My Chinese American friend Millie was brave enough to try one once, and when I asked her for a review, she said it tasted as bad as it smelled, made her very dizzy, and she couldn't really recommend it. Thank the gods for friends like Millie who do

apparently the establishment's by-the-hour customers spew out this stuff with little regard for aim or accuracy. That, at least, would account for the smell of licorice. I beg J. H. to take me somewhere else, but it turns out that this hotel is our only option. I look around with revulsion at the grime, the bold roaches, and a bathroom that probably hasn't been cleaned in a decade. I layer the toilet seat with an inch of paper, refuse to touch the sink, and curl myself into a chair so that my feet are tucked underneath me, which means that the roaches will have to be particularly inventive if they ever hope to scale these heights. I'm furious and terrified and exhausted, but at least I'm full. Lots of scurrying in the walls, shouts from the hallways, and moans through the thin walls combine with the sounds of hawking and spitting. Daylight can't come fast enough, and we catch the first bus out of town.

J. H. FEEDS ME WELL, I have to give him that, both in Taipei and all points south. He puts forth more ideas on the subject of food than I have ever heard of before, plus he has decided that it is his job to fatten me up and train my palate. He introduces me to all his regular haunts our first months together, and these holes-in-the-wall offer very different culinary visions of China once I have this gourmand by my side to do all the ordering. Most of the time, though, we are eating our early dinners at cheap little places that serve the simple

---

all the heavy lifting.

fare found on Taiwan's military bases. Perhaps it's because J. H.'s father is a retired Nationalist Air Force colonel, but my boyfriend's happiest memories seem to center on these homey foods of his childhood, on all the things that equal comfort and family in his mind. As a result, we are dining on little more than vegetables, doufu, and rice, all of which certainly are healthy, as well as decidedly delicious.

Over these meals, J. H. starts to talk about himself, about his childhood, about being sent away to a boys' boarding school because his young mother was overwhelmed with him and his three younger siblings. He tells me stories of life among a tribe of young boys: of climbing up the chimney of an abandoned factory and stripping naked with the others so they could watch their clothes float away under the moonlight, of gluing cutouts of turtles onto flies and dumping them on an unfortunate teacher's desk when his back was turned, of stealing bananas from the groundskeeper's private garden and gorging on them behind a wall, of salting and air-drying the wild birds and fish they caught for after-hour feasts, and of quickly learning to speak Sichuanese like everyone else, for this gave these pint-size inmates the illusion that their world was actually a secret society operating on nothing but little-boy rules. It was *Lord of the Flies* meets *Le Petit Nicolas*. He prides himself on his ability to make me laugh so hard that I cry.

FALLING IN LOVE with a place is in certain respects a lot like falling in love with a person, for both require a certain surrender of the self to the other, a blending of edges, a joining of fates. I often wonder what would have happened to me if not for J. H. Whatever else, I never would have toughed it out in Taiwan long enough to finally speak Mandarin with a modicum of ease, and I most definitely would never have learned to read the language or had any reason at all to remain on the island. But here he is, a part of my life now. He came along, took hold of that slender thread that connected us, and changed everything.

It's hard to believe, but true: J. H. was the first person I met when I landed in Taiwan. "Ah," people sigh when they hear that. "Love at first sight. How sweet."

Anything but. I loathed the man. He made that reaction easy, for the first words out of his mouth were, "Oh, you're the one who hates kids." He was collecting me and the other students at the old Songshan Airport on Taipei's northern outskirts when he said that. Bent almost double under my big army backpack, wearing an olive green unitard with an Equal Rights pendant flopping about, I panted with as much restraint as I could muster that I had merely asked that there be no babies or toddlers in my host family, that I wanted to study quietly without getting roped in as somebody's free babysitter.

"Like I said," he growled, "you're the one who hates kids."

J. H. worked as an administrator at my school, and as far as he was concerned I was just one more in the long line of pain-in-the-butt American college students he had to mollycoddle and spoon-feed. My request, according to him, took ages to satisfy, since all the families on his list had small children and/or babies. So he was not inclined to like me much, either.

A few months later, when his US green card came through, I bid him an offhand farewell and figured I'd never see him again. But a year or so after that, his new job in Long Beach transferred him back to Taipei. Or, I should say, his wife became so completely fed up with her in-laws in California and missed her parents so much that J. H. somehow devised plans to establish a new language school on the outskirts of Taipei, with himself as its director. Despite all this, things deteriorated between him and his wife to the point where she told him she wanted a divorce, and he moved out. Some months later, he met up for coffee with Mike, who was one of his old American students. Since Mike also happened to be one of my buddies, he in turn invited me and somebody else from our school to join in. After a while, Mike and my classmate headed off to do something, and that left J. H. and me sitting across the table from each other, so we called for the check and he said he'd find me a taxi.

We strolled down the street looking for one, but since every cab already had a fare, we just kept on walking and talking. It was a cool evening, perfect weather for a long stroll, and the night sky was a canopy of stars. Or, at least, that's what J. H. says. All I know for sure is that was the first time we ever spoke to each other at any length. I'm told that we discussed politics, literature, philosophy, history, and art. This was, after all, a seven-mile ramble. When J. H. said good-bye that evening, he asked if we could meet over another cup of coffee, and I for some reason said, "Sure, why not?" He called the next morning, and that was the beginning of the end of my life as a loner.

I didn't know what to do with this man. I had enough on my plate with all my existential crises, and I didn't need or want further complications in my life. For one, he was so much older: thirteen years. Plus, he was laden with too much connubial baggage, such as a three-year-old daughter and an unresolved marriage, stuff that I really did not want to deal with at twenty-three. I was also determined not to fall in love. I had so much left to do, like ride the Trans-Siberian Railway to Moscow, hike around Europe, find the perfect man, land the ideal job, and discover what I was meant to do in this life. I kept on telling him it wasn't going to work out. But he wore me down in spite of my objections. J. H. was (and is) the most intelligent person I'd ever met. I loved the sound of his voice and the things he had to teach me, his charisma, his knowledge, his endless stream of talk, his handsome face, and all the fantastic food that he fed me. And then one day I looked at him and in a moment of clarity realized that I was completely smitten.

I HAVE NEVER quite figured out who taught him to eat so well. He can't remember, either, and simply puts it down to osmosis. J. H. could best be described as a gastronomic sponge gifted with a photographic memory and an endless appetite, for he remembers the taste of just about every dish he's ever eaten. He is also a decidedly picky eater, and restaurants annoy him to no end whenever they fail to deliver perfection. So I try cooking for him a number of times—mainly the Western dishes that I know by heart—and while he eats them and helps out in the kitchen as much as he can, I'm picking up more and more hints that he wants me to try my hand at preparing the Chinese dishes he adores.

In the beginning, his strategy was roundabout. We have always adored hanging out in bookstores, for example, and I admit that he might have caught me looking covetously at the fancy bilingual cookbooks by Taiwan's famous television cookshow host, Fu Pei-mei. And so he got me a couple of her books, as well as some by Chen Jianmin and Ma Junquan, and it's quite possible I sat down and deciphered a few of their dishes, and we enjoyed the results. I then moved on to some of the browned and brittle paperbacks he brought back triumphantly from var-

ious used-book stands. But they crumbled pretty quickly, and in any event offered little in the way of allure, for they contained no photographs, no drawings, no details of any sort. Instead, they were written in the terse style of my grandma's recipe cards: Take a chicken, season it, braise it with this and that, cook until it looks right, and there you are.

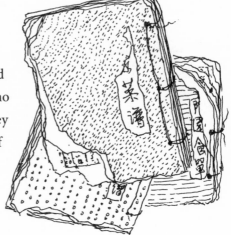

Not only that, but as I fanned through these cookbooks, I felt like he was definitely overestimating my reading abilities. A lot of this had to do with the fact that Chinese and English are nothing alike. Simply put, the logic that designed them and the histories that shaped them and the geography that separated them produced two diametrically different languages. Chinese evolved over five millennia in an isolated land without much input from the rest of the world, so it has its own set of rules, its own inherent logic, and its own way of doing things.

English, on the other hand, is a relatively modern language—a mashup of everything from Old Norse to Greek to Latin to French to German, as well as contributions from whatever traders and invaders interacted with my ancestors. But, as with just about every other language on planet Earth, written English reflects current pronunciation, and that is why the words in *The Canterbury Tales* are nigh on incomprehensible to modern-day Americans. But then again, English has always proven itself to be malleable and open to new ideas, so here and there we have even managed to shoehorn a few Chinese words and phrases into our lexicon—like *typhoon, kumquat, feng shui,* and even *Long time no see*—although the names of Chinese foods tend to be referred to either by their Japanese counterparts (think shiitake and tofu and sake) or else translated into English (as with soy sauce and rice wine). Maybe it's the tones that give us so much trouble. Or it's all those Xs and Zs and Qs and Js that discourage.

Be that as it may, the language of China is now changing rapidly as English travels in the other direction, thanks to American pop—and even culinary—culture. New Chinese words are created all the time as translators race to bring Western ideas to Asia, like *fĕnsī* to describe the fans or groupies who follow a celebrity, *qĭsī* for cheese, *luómànshĭ* to describe romance, *bāshì* to mean bus, *qiăokèlì* and *kāfēi* for chocolate and coffee, *yăpíshì* to mean yuppified, and *Màidāngláo* for McDonald's. English words get sprinkled into everyday conversation now, too, especially by those hoping to impress their television audiences. ("I don't know how to *hold* [keep] my boyfriend." "She is not very *lady* [ladylike]." "He is very *man* [masculine].") But then again, the desire to amaze is probably the whole point of it all. One of my political science professors at the University of Hawaii was guilty of similar pretension when he boomed out lines from *Finnegans Wake* at me whenever the mood struck. ("What did you think of the Watergate hearings?" "Thus the unfacts, did we possess them, are too imprecisely few to warrant our certitude.") More than a tad awestruck at his superior knowledge, I was also terribly confused, yet too insecure ever to risk calling him out as a poseur.

CHINESE MAY APPEAR formidable to our eyes, but it is in many ways much simpler than English. It doesn't have tenses, yet we still manage to grasp the meanings through context ("I earlier eat") or with the judicious addition of a character that tells you this is in the future or past ("Tomorrow I future go to school" and "Last week I write past him a letter"). There are no genders in the spoken language—no *he*, *she*, or *it*—since context will usually supply most of the information we need. And once you think of the four tones in Mandarin as vowel sounds, these immediately become more manageable and easier to imitate.

But that's what is good about the *spoken* dialect I am learning: Mandarin. On the more difficult end of the scale, I am faced with the fact that written Chinese possesses no alphabet but rather is composed of square characters I am expected to memorize individually. Most of these suggest a thought or concept, instead of simply telling you how to pronounce them. One of the most brilliant things about a language designed this way is that these characters have allowed China to remain China for all of recorded history, with its people bound together by their unique written language. Things could have easily taken a wildly different direction, though, if China had ever resorted to an alphabet, for about two hundred dialects are spoken there. If they had all been written out phonetically, the country might have ended up as linguistically diverse as Europe.

And as if all this were not enough, Chinese was traditionally read from right to left, although in modern times it is most often written from left to right. The script can be arranged vertically or horizontally, depending upon the mood of the writer and the formality of the document and whether it was written on the Mainland or elsewhere. What this means as a practical matter is that even before I try to read something, I first have to figure out the direction of the characters. But wait, there's more: In older classical writings, punctuation doesn't exist, so reading sometimes becomes a bit like one of those find-a-word games in the back of the Sunday supplement. Up, down, left, right, no punctuation, no alphabet, no mercy. That first year, I stared at a block of four characters in a temple in downtown Taipei that looked sort of like this:

I asked the Chinese girl next to me how I should know which way the characters were meant to be read. "You just have to figure it out," she shrugged. "You know, whichever way makes sense."

To make matters worse, J. H. speaks Mandarin with such a perfect, sophisticated accent that he sounds like a Chinese version of David Attenborough, which would explain why he used to work as a radio news announcer. My Mandarin during our first few years together must have sounded like fingernails on a chalkboard to him, because once the newness of our relationship had lost its sheen, he began ~~determinedly criticizing~~ gently correcting the way I spoke. Before he came along, I was definitely of the mind that tones didn't matter, that they were optional and, frankly, more than a bit arbitrary and irksome. I didn't realize how important these tones were until I heard the American head of our language program give an address in Chinese. The flat monotone of his Mandarin was so abysmal that I immediately realized it must be what I sounded like, too.

That being said, my boyfriend's world continues to mystify me. True, I catch the drift of most conversations and, if I manage to keep my sassy asides carefully locked up, I usually can make it through the evening without totally embarrassing myself, but double meanings, the Chinese sense of humor, cultural references, and deeper ideas whiz right by me.

He notices, and it worries him. Taipei is still very much home to a traditional Chinese way of living, with few foreigners ever sighted outside the colleges and the Tianmu District's expat enclave. Yet he wants me to be accepted as an actual member of the tribe despite my appearance. He looks pained whenever I misspeak some Chinese phrase, or when I get a tone wrong and thus end up saying something particularly stupid. It's exhausting, and as a result I am extremely tense. But he has a point. I won't learn fast and well if my entire self is not pushed and dragged into his world, for otherwise I will be seen as alien, as The Other, as someone to be indulged or sidelined.

We are therefore attempting to bridge this cultural and linguistic divide, albeit with mixed results.

The first son and very pampered child of  well-placed parents with distinctive backgrounds, J. H. was raised to be unusually class conscious. But I have hopes for him. He is softening at the edges and dialing down the pomposity. He listens. He helps clean the apartment. He carries my basket as I shop for groceries. He proudly holds my hand no matter the company, and he runs interference when needed. Nevertheless, he really doesn't know what to do with me now that we've fallen in love. White girls aren't settling down with Chinese guys in Taiwan at this point in time. We have no template to work from. I simply don't fit into either his life or this society.

Seeking the path of least resistance, we start with the food and the language, and then work up from there.

Coffee Gelée (V)

KĀFĒI DÒNG 咖啡凍

J. H. loves ice cream more than anyone I know, but I've found that I can make him quite happy with substitutes if they are as delicious as this one. Coffee gelée is such an inspired yet easy sweet that I often wonder why it isn't on every menu in town.

2 cups | 500 ml cool water

5 envelopes | 35 g powdered gelatin

4 cups | 1 liter very hot, very strong espresso or coffee (regular or decaf)

Sweetened condensed milk, as desired

Pour the cool water into a shallow 8-cup | 2-liter baking dish. Sprinkle the gelatin over the water and stir it around as it softens, while breaking up any lumps. Gently stir in the hot coffee until the gelatin is completely dissolved. Let cool to room temperature, then cover and refrigerate for a couple of hours, until the coffee gelée has solidified.

Just before serving, cut the gelatin into cubes. Scoop them into glass cups or bowls, then drizzle the condensed milk over the top. *Makes 6 cups | 1.5 liters, about 12 servings.*

Tips

This is an ideal place to use up that jar of instant espresso that's been hogging space in the back of your cupboard. Just make it stronger than directed on the label.

Some folks are averse to sweetened condensed milk. I am definitely not one of them, but those who are can pour sweetened heavy cream over the gelée and still find themselves very happy.

Bear Paw Doufu (V)

XIŌNGZHĂNG DÒUFŬ 熊掌豆腐

This delightfully simple, utterly delicious recipe for doufu is gently adapted from one by the late Chen Jianmin, personal chef to Taiwan's most renowned artist, Chang Dai-chien. He was also the father of Chen Kennichi, the virtually invincible Iron Chef Chinese on the original Japanese program.

Perhaps it's because I knew Master Chang from my work at Taipei's National Museum of History that I've always felt I had a tentative sort of tie to Chef Chen. But then again, it might be because I've cooked so many of his dishes with success. Both Master Chang and Chef Chen were from Sichuan, yet while this classic home-style recipe can boast terrific texture and flavor contrasts, it doesn't have even a whisper of chiles or Sichuan peppercorns hiding inside.

I'm not exactly sure where the name came from, but one story is that the Tang Xuanzong emperor made a royal tour to Sichuan, where the people were so poor that they didn't know what to serve his majesty, so a clever but nameless chef invented this recipe and said it was made with the rare delicacy known as bears' paws. When the emperor tasted it, he laughed with delight, and the cook lived to see another day, and the dish can still be enjoyed a thousand years later.

2 (19-ounce | 539-g) blocks tender or silken bean curd

1 winter bamboo shoot (about 2 ounces | 50 g), fresh or frozen

6 dried black mushrooms, soaked overnight in cool water

4 green onions

¼ cup | 20 g peeled and thinly sliced fresh ginger

Oil for frying

4 cups | 1 liter unsalted or low-sodium mushroom, chicken, or
   pork stock

¼ cup | 60 ml Shaoxing rice wine

3 tablespoons regular Chinese soy sauce

A few grinds of black pepper

1 teaspoon sugar

Slice the bean curd crosswise into 9 pieces, then cut each of these in half so that you have 18 squares. Set these in a single layer on a kitchen towel to absorb most of the moisture while you prepare the rest of the ingredients, and pat the tops dry while you're at it.

If you are using a frozen bamboo shoot, simply defrost it. If you're using a fresh bamboo shoot, peel it, trim off any hard bits, and cut it in half, then place it in a small saucepan, cover it with water, and simmer until tender; drain well. Remove the mushrooms from the soaking liquid (strain and reserve the liquid) and slice the mushroom caps into thin pieces. Thinly slice the bamboo shoot. Chop the green onions and slice the ginger into thin strips.

Pour 1 inch | 2 cm of oil into a wok and heat over medium heat until hot. Slide in half of the bean curd and fry, stirring gently, until the squares are golden brown all over. Remove the fried bean curd with chopsticks or a spatula to a bowl and repeat with the rest of the bean curd.

Pour most of the oil out of the wok and set it back over high heat. Add the green onions, ginger, bamboo shoots, and mushrooms and toss in the hot oil until the mushrooms start to brown. Pour in the reserved soaking liquid and the stock, then add the fried bean curd, wine, soy sauce, and pepper. Bring the liquid to a boil, cover, and simmer for about 10 minutes, then remove the lid and continue to simmer the bean curd until only a slick of the stock remains.

Add the sugar and adjust the seasoning as needed, then arrange the ingredients on a rimmed platter. Serve with hot rice and maybe a vegetable, if you're feeling energetic. *Serves 4 to 6.*

Tips

Use regular doufu if you can't find tender or silken bean curd, and this will still taste delicious. If you live in an area where doufu is hard to find, be on the lookout for vacuum-packed versions whenever you do visit a Chinatown or larger Asian grocery store, for these do not need to be refrigerated, have a fairly long shelf life, and in fact are simply stored on grocery shelves. Packed in small aseptic paper boxes much like chicken stock, these are mainly produced in Japan by companies like Mori-nu.

Bamboo shoots truly are best if they are fresh or frozen, but they can be almost impossible to find outside of areas with larger Chinese populations. Canned is an option, but I never like these because they taste of the can and little else. If you like them, though, by all means use them. Or, just don't add bamboo shoots to this recipe—it will still manage to be very tasty.

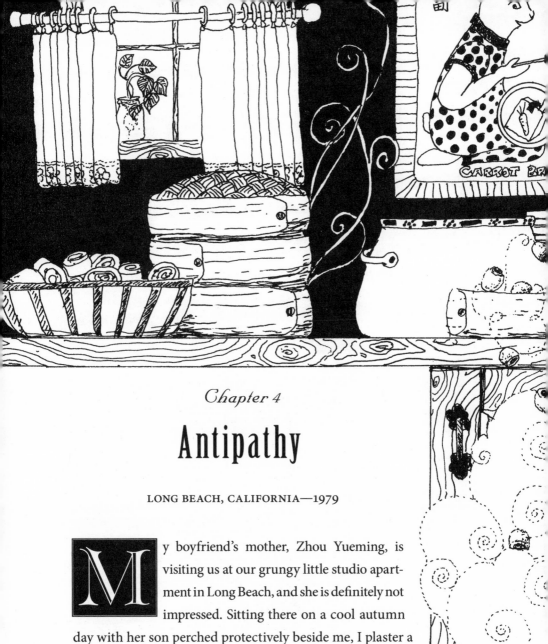

Chapter 4

Antipathy

LONG BEACH, CALIFORNIA—1979

M y boyfriend's mother, Zhou Yueming, is
visiting us at our grungy little studio apartment in Long Beach, and she is definitely not
impressed. Sitting there on a cool autumn
day with her son perched protectively beside me, I plaster a
welcoming smile on my face and try to look delighted to see
her as I pour some oolong tea into our mismatched mugs.

She scans the place with hooded eyes, giving monosyllabic responses in her very northern accent to my intensely chipper little queries in tortured Mandarin while strenuously avoiding even the merest glance in my direction. She is very obviously mystified as to why she has to be in such a cheap dive, why her eldest son should be letting her down so completely, and most of all why she has to be confronted with the impossibly foreign girlfriend he recently brought back with him from Taiwan.

No guidelines exist on the proper way to weasel into a potential Chinese mother-in-law's good graces, and I'm foundering in the dark. I offer her some candies and nuts, but they cannot be expected to wield much magic here. For that, I have to wait another ten minutes, until the contents of the bamboo baskets steaming away on our chipped Wedgewood stove will save me. Or not. The problem is, I have no idea what is going to happen. I am only certain that she thoroughly dislikes me. No, *dislike* is much too mild a word for what's going on here. My mind runs over as many escalating verbs as I can remember, while the other half of my brain fretfully attempts to come up with something clever to say during those long, awkward silences. I realize now that I should have known better than to take her dislike, distaste, opposition, aversion, hostility, abhorrence, repugnance, hatred, loathing, detestation, repulsion, and utter antipathy for me as something personal.

It is not that hard to see it from her point of view. After all, if I were on the outside looking in, I'd readily agree that I am definitely a miserable candidate for number-one daughter-in-law. I have no social connections, no illustrious lineage, and no fame or fortune to rec-

ommend me. And, the worst of all,
I am so obviously one
hundred percent white.

As if all that were
not enough, it should be
mentioned that J. H. is
still officially married to
his first wife. Even though he
moved out quite a while back, she
has changed her mind and is now not at all
interested in a divorce,* so their little daughter has been pleading with
him to wait until she gets out of school before they formally split. I'm
therefore just the live-in girlfriend while things shake out, a situation
that will remain in place for close to two decades. A few months after
he moved himself, a bag of clothes, a camera, and a stack of books
into my Taipei apartment, his American company told him to return
to Long Beach so that he could plan a formal Mandarin language
program at Soochow University near the National Palace Museum in

---

* In Taiwan at this point, whenever a couple filed for divorce, fathers were inevitably
awarded full custody of their sons and daughters, and mothers could even be barred by
their ex-husbands from ever seeing their children again. The threat of this, of course,
was used by rather unscrupulous men (and their parents) to force these women into
putting up with way more than they ever should have. And even though J. H. willingly
gave everything of value to his wife, including custody of their daughter, her fears were
nevertheless terrifyingly understandable. Not that this made me very happy or gar-
nered me the slightest bit of sympathy from J. H.'s mother or her daughters.

Taipei. He insisted that I come back to the States with him, ostensibly to meet his family and to somehow wrangle my proper place in the Huang hierarchy. He said they'd love me once they got to know me.

Yeah, right.

He's so much older that he was in college when I started kindergarten. He has a daughter whom he loves more than anything in the world. My Chinese-language abilities are laughably minimal. I quit college a few degrees short of graduating with a 3.85 average because I just couldn't see the point of continuing. I have no marketable skills. Kids don't even make a guest appearance on my bucket list.

The thing is, in this Chinese family, any one of these qualities would be reason enough to get voted off the short list, but hey, I'm an overachiever.

At this point, you might be thinking I may have bit off more than I could chew.

You would be right.

THE FIRST THING you need to know about J. H.'s mother is that she has a very high opinion of herself. She lives in such a rarefied realm that she has no friends—she cuts people out of her life for the merest infractions, at least as far as I can see.

Her life is confined to her immediate family: her two daughters and their children, as well as her two sons. She and J. H.'s dad have lived apart for many years, but his father still manages to make guest appearances at the family get-togethers whenever he's in the area. And these are the only people she thinks about all the time, without exception. For many years now, her main concern has been that there are no male heirs to the Huang name. And because J. H.'s relationship with his Taiwanese wife started to crumble around the time their daughter was born, his mother has focused her considerable energies on finding her younger son the right girl, a Northern Chinese one this time around, a sweet young thing who will bear her the grandsons she so badly wants. A few years ago, when she lived up in Fairbanks with her older daughter, the pickings were particularly slim—so poor in fact that as soon as she heard news of an eligible young lady down in Anchorage, she bought a round-trip ticket and flew eight hundred miles for no other reason than to check her out. Now that she's moved into the home near Long Beach of her younger daughter, Little Three,* you might think that the massive Chinese population of greater Los Angeles County would be able to cough up a contender or two for the title of Miss Perfect. Alas, none have as yet passed muster. These are, indeed, desperate times.

It became such an obsession that not even breast cancer could slow her down. While recovering in the hospital from surgery, her

* J. H.'s parents at one time called him Little Dragon, for boys are sometimes given family nicknames that reflect the lunar years in which they were born. (Actually, J. H. was born in the Year of the Snake, but since snakes are thought of as miniature dragons in Chinese culture, a son born in that year tends to be called Little Dragon, a definite improvement on being known as a little snake.) This is the same reason why his brother—the youngest child—has always been known to the family as Little Ox. The two daughters in the middle, though, received the more feminine names of Little Two and Little Three, while J. H. called his daughter Little Cowgirl, since, like her uncle, she was born in the Year of the Ox.

younger son went to visit her. His normally robust mother looked pale and wan. She was hooked up to beeping machines and unable to speak. She appeared at death's door. Her baby boy clasped her cold hand in his and bent toward her, remorseful at long last for his carefree ways.

"Ma," Little Ox whispered, "whenever you feel better, I want you to find me a good girl."

She checked out the next day.

STILL QUITE OBLIVIOUS to all this, as well as to my role in this drama, I have invited my boyfriend's mother over to feed her, to get to know her, and to give her a chance to know me.

Her given name, Yueming, is composed of the characters for *moon* plus *bright*. Nevertheless, she blames this name for all of her bad luck: "My fate is like that of the moon: waxing and waning, up and down, light and dark, with very few full days," she sighs whenever her life seems especially bleak. One son-in-law gave her the English name of Gloria, but few people ever called her that, so I'll refer to her here by the name I was instructed to call her: Elder Paternal Aunt, or *Bómǔ*, which sounds like we've become really close, almost blood relatives, but that's what you're supposed to call any woman who is older than your parents. In other words, this is nothing but a generic title, one that holds me at an indisputably firm distance and underscores the nonexistence of any actual relationship.

At this point, though, I remain totally clueless as to why she hates me so much. Instead, I'm in a happy haze of denial as I refill the teapot and fuss around with some plates on the counter. With my back to her, I fantasize that I'll somehow find a way to charm my way into obtaining at least a smidgen of acceptance from this imperious woman. And then I turn around to see her glowering away at the table and think, *Well, maybe not.*

At this point, I do happen to have one arrow left in my quiver, one that has never let me down: I love to cook. In fact, over the past couple of months, I've gotten pretty adept at her son's care and feeding. Part of this improvement is definitely due to his hovering over me at the stove, sniffing and tasting and adding and advising. The first few times we cooked together in Taipei, he usually commandeered the kitchen and shooed me away unless he wanted to show me something important, such as how to flatten a duck or the correct way to toss stuff in a wok. I was left to do all the grunt work at the dining table, like snapping water spinach to this unrepentant Virgo's precise specifications (*Make sure there is only one leaf per segment*) and slicing green onions into precise slivers (*They should be no wider than a toothpick*) and cutting eggplants into precise wedges (*Be sure to blanch them before they oxidize*) and stringing snow peas precisely from both ends so that not a fiber remains (*Don't forget to soak them in ice water so they crisp up*). Dinner took forever. I was chained to the galley, and his overriding preoccupation with tidiness meant he had to clean each bowl, wipe every counter, and sweep the floor before he proceeded to the next dish.

Within a few days, rebellion was fomenting in the ranks and mutiny was in the air. This wasn't at all what I had signed up for. Besides, it was my kitchen. I finally chased him out and reclaimed my wok stove, telling him that it was his turn to prep the veggies to his heart's content, and by the way, he gets to wash the dishes, too. I was a little surprised when he gave in easily. But then again, he is such a devout student of Sun-tzu that

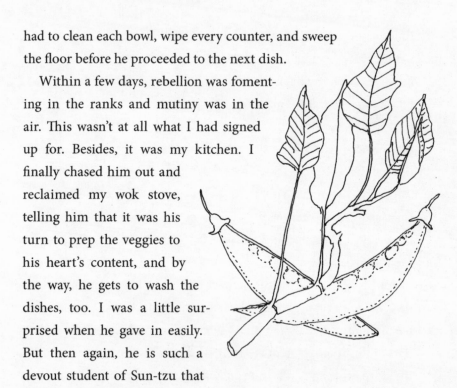

he eventually wrote a popular edition of *The Art of War*, so perhaps this was all part of some Machiavellian plot to get me to do the cooking. I wouldn't put it past him.

The other source for my newfound abilities in the kitchen is the collection of Chinese-language cookbooks we've been amassing both here and back in Taipei. Almost as soon as we moved into our little 1930s-era furnished studio in a decidedly working-class corner of Long Beach, we brought home a box full of recently published Mainland paperbacks we had come across in an LA Chinatown bookstore on High Street. The set I have come to love the most bears the very basic title of *Zhōngguó shípǔ*, which simply means these small paperbacks are, literally, Chinese cookbooks. Stacked in pride of place near the kitchen door, their pastel covers envelop newsprint so cheap that it is already foxing after only a year or two. Printed in tiny, eye-straining type, they are bound with staples along the spine that are already rusting when we buy them. But in spite of their appearance, these are the deep dives we have been seeking, for they offer gastronomic insights into parts of China that we haven't been able to find anyplace else, and each slim volume is devoted to a different province's cuisine.

This set, while undeniably opening new doors and sparking my interest in cooking to no small degree, has proved to be more than formidable because it was printed in simplified Chinese, and I had only learned the traditional characters in college and on Taiwan. Plus, they contain cooking concepts and terms and characters that are utterly unfamiliar. Specialized words appear for such things as culinary techniques employed only in certain parts of the country, while unheard-of ingredients show up in one volume— sometimes for just one recipe—and then disappear. And, as if things were not difficult enough for me, enigmatic historical references have been tossed in, apparently to lend certain recipes heft and importance. But these books also tell me things like the proper name for each cut of

火爪
火膧
雌爿
雄爿
中腰峰
筒骨
下腰峰
千斤骨
火码

a Jinhua ham, how to make the basic sauces that local cooks once relied on for their signature flavors, the proper names for each area's poultry and fish, and all the minutiae that sets each region's foods apart from the rest. I therefore have come to think of them as my new textbooks.

The good news is that these cookbooks seem as if they will work to my advantage, for J. H.'s mother has had little opportunity to dine on dishes from her North China home since she moved to the States from Taiwan. Few regional restaurants as yet exist in Southern California, and therefore the clan's feasting tends to take place mainly in one or another of greater Los Angeles's Cantonese dining palaces that feature the glorious foods of South China, where our upcoming dinner lazes around in gigantic tanks above our table and shiny lacquered ducks hang in windows before being whacked up and served on massive white platters. These are expensive outings for us, but J. H. longs to be a part of his family, so we do our best to tag along whenever we have a few extra bucks in our pockets. We all pile into his youngest sister's van—me stuffed in the back with Little Three's baby daughter, as far away from his mother as I can manage—and drive over to San Gabriel Valley. The ever-lively Chinese grapevine keeps tabs on what places have opened, who the chefs are, how long the lines will be, what specialties they offer, and how much everything will cost, so the clan hears of things, takes notes, and makes plans. We enthusiastically search out new places to eat, and by *we* I mean *they*. I'm literally only along for the ride.

As Southern California's Asian population continues to grow in the San Gabriel Valley around the formerly sleepy communities of Monterey Park and Alhambra, so does its thick forest of restaurants.

New immigrants flood in from Taiwan and Hong Kong, and soon the first trickles from the Mainland start to color the food scene even more. So many places open up every week that the rivalry is frantically intense at times. But few are ever as fancy as the Cantonese palaces where we dine these days. Crystal chandeliers, walls of saltwater tanks filled with fish and shrimp and lobster and crab, gigantic paintings of peonies and galloping horses, gilded gods offering their blessings, and flocked wallpaper spattered with specks of fat decorate these cavernous dining halls.

J. H.'s family members devour the meals with gusto at times like this, and I revel in these temporary ceasefires in the war against my presence when the only sound at our table is that of eating. Shreds of poached chicken are dipped in salty oils seasoned with ginger and green onions, while precise squares of roast suckling pig perch on savory soybeans. Everyone dives into plates of massive steamed prawns with roe still clasped between their tiny legs or coral-hued crabs studded with black beans and chopped garlic. Any ladylike pretenses are set aside as J. H.'s mother demolishes more food than anyone. Her appetite is nothing short of fierce, and the growing heaps of shells and bones in front of her dare

us to keep up. During these feasts, she actually smiles and joins in whatever jokes are being told. Granted, she doesn't look in my direction very often, but I'm not complaining.

A large steamed fish inevitably arrives toward the end of the meal, normally a freshly killed rock cod spangled with shredded green onions and ginger, its sauce a restrained mixture of soy sauce and oil. Everyone in the family loves fried rice and noodles, so the final dish is a mammoth mound of one or the other to satisfy any unfilled crannies lurking in our digestive systems.

Dessert is on the house: a sweet soup of tapioca or mung beans or red beans, sometimes with coconut milk and other times with sweetened condensed milk or cured tangerine peel, while during the long Southern California summer it might be decorated with colorful melon confetti. The signal that it's time to leave arrives in the form of another gift: a huge plate of orange wedges or sliced watermelon, just a little something in case we are still hungry or haven't managed to take the hint yet. We eat until we find it hard to walk, and we wrap up the leftovers for his mother or sister. I anxiously peel off a couple of twenties as our contribution to the meal, knowing that we will have to eat frugally for the rest of the week if we're going to stay afloat.

It's all utterly delicious, and yet it all is so downright nerve-racking.

THE GOOD NEWS is that his mother cheers up considerably when she is full. This must be a congenital trait, for I have discovered that feeding J. H. his childhood favorites is the easiest way to make him happy. Before he came along, I had never seen such a strong connection between eating and mood.

I start to connect the dots: like mother, like son.

However, the second thing you have to know about his mother is that even if I do find that edible Proustian key to her psyche, this tough little cookie won't crumble very easily. She is as notoriously closemouthed about herself as a Cold War spy. Up until this point, she hasn't even told anyone what year she was born, for she believes that if the gods don't realize how old she is, they'll forget to schedule her death. All I am sure of is that once upon a time she was born many decades ago on the sixth day of the twelfth lunar month, and that she grew up in the northern seaport of Tianjin as the pampered little daughter of a warlord.

Nevertheless, I pester my boyfriend for more clues, and one day he mentions that, as a little girl, she had loved to eat the steamed little chestnut thimbles called *lìzi wōwōtóuer*. When a tattered Chinese memoir tells me that such pastries had also been a favorite of the Dowager Empress Cixi, I can't help but make a few inappropriate connections in my mind between the famed old lady who had once terrorized the Forbidden Palace and the one who is so nonchalantly intimidating me now. We flip through those old cookbooks in search of more things she might like, and before long I have managed to master a handful of dishes from North China that I think just might be the ticket, including those thimbles. Rich brown, slightly sweet, and naturally smoky in aroma, they are fashioned out of dried Chinese chestnuts—in other words, a half-pound of hard little nuggets that have to be soaked, painstakingly peeled, steamed, and then finely ground up by hand into a paste before being mixed with flour and

leavening. They are a labor of love—
or, if not love, then at least a desperate longing for acceptance.

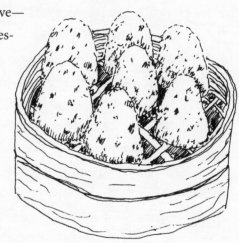

And so on this morning,
with two baskets of these
thimbles steaming behind me
on the stove, I consider myself
armed and ready for an audience with my boyfriend's
mother. More carefully honed
weapons from North China are
set out in this battle array: two dozen
buttery sesame cookies, a large pot of creamy sweet walnut soup, and
a red-cooked chicken with mounds of black mushrooms and mealy
potatoes just in case she stays long enough for dinner, plus a pyra-
mid of homemade steamed buns rolled up into twists around specks
of green onions, dry-fried sesame seeds, and ground toasted Sichuan
peppercorns. I have organized my master plan down to the last detail
almost as if it were the invasion of Normandy. Now I just need those
starchy little thimbles and their backups to flip the right switches in
her mind.

As she sits there at my kitchen table this afternoon, aromatic ten-
drils from the bamboo steamer begin to attract her attention. She
sniffs the air and keeps looking toward the stove. Even though she
won't deign to ask me what I'm making, I feel the first small glim-
mers of hope.

I busy myself in the kitchen, since my conversational abilities are
not about to win me any points. I sneak a peek at their profiles as

they sit across the table from each other and realize that J. H. indeed resembles his mother so much it's almost frightening . . . the same brow, the same shape of the head, the same half-moons under the eyes, the same flat space above the same distinctive nose. No wonder that cook in Donggang recognized him as his mother's son. Even their physiques are similar—they have the athletic bodies of Northerners, unlike the svelte Cantonese bones of his father. In old black-and-white photos from the Mainland, his mother looks like a Chinese version of Ava Gardner. Unlike her son's eyes, though, hers are long and striking, and her mouth is set, at least today, in a humorless straight line.

I continue to glance over at her surreptitiously, taking advantage of the attention she's paying to her son as they chat. Her black hair is graying beautifully, a white stripe arching back from her forehead, almost skunklike in perfection. She wraps her shoulder-length mane in a simple bun now and forgoes makeup and jewelry, dressing down in cheap cotton blouses and gray vests, rather than the high-collared Chinese dresses she used to wear. In spite of that, her beauty remains, her skin smooth and barely wrinkled. I once asked J. H. why she didn't have a wedding ring, and he said she pawned it in order to buy an expensive dictionary. And yet we've never seen her read, not even the newspaper. I mull that thought over and find it to be yet another bizarre puzzle piece I can't quite jimmy into the overall picture.

THE TIMER GOES OFF and I open one of the steamer baskets as I set it before her. Elder Paternal Aunt's eyes sparkle when she recognizes the pastries of her childhood. She plucks one with her chopsticks, bites into it, and lets out an appreciative little sigh. It could be the steam turning the room balmier, but it could also be the taste and memory that make her just a few degrees happier. She breathes down the first thimble in an instant, and I press more on her, reveling in the sudden thaw. Her body relaxes as she eats, and I refill her teacup.

As we nibble our way through the rest of the first round, I tentatively ratchet up my courage to join in their conversation. The rapid disappearance of those little lumps suggests they are something she hasn't enjoyed for a very long time, so I ask his mother when she last ate them. In her own mother's home, she replies, which would have been forty years ago. She tells us a bit about her upbringing back in Tianjin, which serves as Beijing's seaport—sort of like Long Beach to Los Angeles, if you are looking for convenient parallels to this story. To get an idea of when all this is taking place, I ask her when she was born. In 1922, she says quickly while looking away. And over the next couple of hours, her life begins to spill out in steady increments, turning this into the one time her son hears her speak at length about what happened so long ago, of her fabulous beginnings and her family's swift fall from grace.

As an only child, Elder Paternal Aunt grew up surrounded by adults, she said, mainly her mother, maternal grandmother, and three uncles, as well as a cadre of servants. Her father, Zhou Zhongxiang, hailed from rural Yunnan, a rugged province that lies almost thirteen hundred miles from Tianjin on the southern edge of China between Sichuan and Tibet, and bordered by Vietnam, Laos, and Myanmar (Burma). He was just an infrequent visitor to their home, but even so, having this man as her father meant she lived the life of royalty, with both a chauffeur and a nanny who served her and her alone.

"So, *Lǎoyé* [Maternal Grandpa] was a warlord from Yunnan, right? And he worked under yet another warlord while he lived in Tianjin?" J. H. asks his mother. This had been the great family legend, one that in turn lent his descendants the smack of status, romance, and history.

She pauses, looks at the table, and replies, "You could say so." Her son's eyebrows knit in slight confusion, but Elder Paternal Aunt continues the story of her childhood, overriding any pauses that would require her to stop and explain.

You may be thinking to yourself, "Wait, what did she mean by 'You could say so?'" And, "If he was from Yunnan, what was he doing that far north?" And, "If his boss was a warlord, what did that make him?" These were questions that bothered me, too, for years.

And I'll get to them eventually. For now, though, let's return to her side of the story.

Elder Paternal Aunt grew up in her mother's hometown of Tianjin. But it was far from a pleasant nuclear family where Dad came home at the end of a hard day's work. Instead, her father was often away on duty, as he operated under the command of that powerful Yunnanese boss. Her father was the officially adopted godson of this general, which accorded him status much like that of a son, for the relationship between a godfather and his godson in traditional China was almost akin to a blood relationship. They both were from the same region, and added together such close bonds had allowed her father to become one of the warlord's chief lieutenants. A job like this came with very nice perks, such as receiving his monthly salary in the form of gold leaves stacked on a lacquer tray wrapped in red silk and delivered by one of the boss's beautifully dressed servant girls.

Over the second basket of chestnut pastries, Elder Paternal Aunt expands on her story. She talks about being the sole child of a man who eventually abandoned his little family when he did not get the boy he demanded. Her parents had not had the luxury of a love match, of course. Rather, it was an arrangement made by J. H.'s great-grandfather for his only daughter. And as is true throughout much of the world, the purpose of this union was to produce sons, and a cute little daughter was definitely not going to cut the mustard. Elder Paternal Aunt's eyes flash as she remembers the guilt and anger she felt at having been born a mere girl. I murmur something consoling and most likely incredibly feeble while I serve her a plate of hot cookies and portion out the gently sweet soup.

While nibbling on these, she remembers someone saying that

her father had eventually taken on yet another young wife after leaving them—or maybe it was a concubine, she muses—who finally bore him that sought-after male heir. He was so proud that he had his troops paraded in front of him and that long-awaited son cradled in his mother's arms. Not long after that, Elder Paternal Aunt's father was shot by one of his own men during an insurrection. No one knows for certain what happened to the body, or to the young mother, or even to the infant son.

THE LIGHT IN our apartment starts to fade as I heat up the chicken and buns. I can see my thoughts reflected in my boyfriend's face as he digests this news about the possibility of an uncle being out there somewhere. I continue to feed her food from her past as she feeds us her memories.

J. H. suddenly looks up and asks what happened then to *Lǎolǎo*, his maternal grandmother, the only one of his grandparents he ever met. He spent time with her just once when he was about five and his father was stationed in Beijing after the war. Since Tianjin is only about a hundred miles away to the east, his grandmother traveled by train for a short visit. J. H. immediately adored her, and from all accounts *Lǎolǎo* turned out to be the one person in his childhood who appears to have unreservedly adored him, too. Her dark hair was combed smoothly back from her broad forehead, he remembers, framing a pair of kind, intelligent eyes. Everything about her was precise and perfect, including the beautifully embroidered slippers that encased her "three-inch golden lotuses"—incredibly tiny bound feet not much larger than a child's fist—that poked out from under her dark silk skirt.

A cloud crosses his mother's face at the thought of her father's assassination. "It was dangerous," she says. "*We* were in danger," she corrects herself. "We had to run. We had to hide. If the soldiers had found us, we would have been killed, too. Or worse."* Her voice

* The Beiyang warlords in northern China had been training highly disciplined troops in Xiaozhan near Tianjin for a couple of decades, but by the mid-1920s this had declined to the point that their foot soldiers were robbing the already impoverished local population of their food. In a wildly misguided attempt to stop this sort of thing, J. H.'s grandmother told her daughter that Xiaozhan's military commanders punished the thieves by publicly gutting them. While this may have served to more or less appease the civilians, it enraged the remaining troops to such an extent that they took their revenge on any officers they could find, including the officers' families.

drops to almost a whisper. "We abandoned our house and stayed out of sight. Everything we had was gone. We had to start all over."

Left to her own devices for the first time in her life, Elder Paternal Aunt tells us, her mother discovered something strong inside herself. With no one to turn to and no place that could house her and her child, she somehow began running a shipping warehouse in Tianjin. Oddly enough, she prospered with this newfound freedom and became a successful businesswoman. She was in charge of a depository full of men, even though her family had deliberately kept her illiterate, restricting her ability to learn even the simplest things with the same finality that they had crushed her heels, broken her tiny toes, and snapped the arches of her feet in two. This new career fed her small family, which still included *Lăolăo*'s younger brothers and mother. She remade herself into her household's breadwinner, and a surprisingly able one at that. However, good luck in her life was consistently followed by bad. Because she was unschooled, she had to hire a bookkeeper to keep track of things on her behalf, and that gave this man the opportunity to embezzle all of her money, leaving her once again destitute. A while later, things began looking up when she married a banker named Mr. Zhang, but then he died and she was left a widow once again. And that is the sum of what Elder Paternal Aunt told us about her mother, who died far away in Tianjin in 1979.

As she reaches out and refills my cup, I do not know whether I am more shocked by the senseless cruelties in her story or by the fact that J. H.'s mother has just now actually served me tea. She takes a sip and continues.

The feudal ways were finally disappearing in China, and her mother wanted to see Elder Paternal Aunt walk and even run with ease—simple pleasures that she, of course, had never enjoyed. However, *Lǎolǎo*'s mother was insisting that the beastly practice of foot binding be inflicted on her granddaughter, for she believed this was the only way to ensure her a good husband. But the times had changed. The child's father was dead. The child's mother was beginning to taste freedom. Women were talking about living lives of their own, going to college, choosing their own mates, and even getting the vote. Independence was in the air. And so Elder Paternal Aunt was the first girl in her family in who knows how many generations to escape foot binding. When she tells us this, J. H.'s mother looks down proudly at her small, perfectly formed feet encased in beaded slippers. I slide my size tens protectively under my chair as I realize my clodhoppers have most likely already been added to the long list of my personal defects and serious shortcomings.

As she slows her storytelling, it becomes clear that Elder Paternal Aunt never managed to leave China—and especially her hometown—behind. There was too much unsettled business back there in Tianjin that still had to be addressed, processed, and perhaps even forgiven. And then, by never bothering to learn to drive or speak much English or even make a friend or two here, she had managed to keep America a distant notion safely beyond her family's walls—that is, at least, until I came along.

Slowly unraveling herself from her memories, she finishes the last of her dinner. We empty our cups. She has run out of words to put to her thoughts. She looks much frailer than I have ever seen her, but the disapproving crease between her eyebrows has softened. As we say our good-byes, I give her a tiny hug that at first makes her freeze. Then, she tentatively squeezes me back before her son drives her home.

Garlic Roast Chicken

SUÀNZI KǍOJĪ 蒜子烤雞

This is my super-easy riff on the red-cooked chicken Elder Paternal Aunt used to love, although I'm being rather subversive here, since both Taiwanese soy paste and Cantonese oyster sauce are Southern Chinese condiments.

Try the super-easy way to peel garlic using your microwave, as described in the Tip below—it's brilliant, though I can't claim to have invented it. Sticking all of those cloves of garlic under the bird's skin may seem fussy at first glance, but they prop up the skin so that it can crisp while they perfume the meat. Plus, the garlic becomes as sweet as candy, especially the cloves under the breast skin. The juice, when it has been chilled, turns into an astoundingly delicious gelée that I can't stop eating. I simply adore everything about this recipe.

1 whole head garlic
1 free-range, organic, or kosher roasting chicken (about 5 pounds | 2.25 kg)
1 bunch green onions, trimmed
½ cup | 125 ml soy paste or oyster sauce

Place an oven rack in the bottom third of the oven and another one just below that. Line a baking sheet with foil and place it on the lower rack to catch any spattering. Preheat the oven to 425°F | 220°C while you prepare the bird. Select a roasting pan that will hold the chicken snugly and has sides at least 2 inches | 5 cm high.

For a suggestion on how to peel the garlic cloves effortlessly, see the Tip below. Wipe the bird dry inside and out with paper towels. Fold the wings under themselves. Stuff the green onions into the bird's cavity. Use your fingers to carefully separate the skin over the breast and thighs from the meat. Slide the peeled garlic evenly under the skin. Don't truss the legs, just leave them sprawling open.

Set the bird into the roasting pan and then on the oven rack. Roast for about 15 minutes, then turn down the heat to 375°F | 190°C, without opening the oven door. After a total of 30 minutes, brush some of the paste or sauce over the chicken, being sure to coat the breast area thoroughly. Then continue roasting, basting the chicken every 15 minutes or so with the paste or sauce and then the juices. The chicken is done when an instant-read thermometer stuck in the thigh reaches 165°F | 75°C, about 60 to 75 minutes. The sugar in the paste or sauce will blacken on the skin by this time, but don't be alarmed, as it will still taste delicious. Remove the bird from the oven, tent a piece of foil over it, and let it rest uncovered for at least 30 minutes.

To serve, discard the green onions and skim the fat from the pan juices, if you like. Gently tear the chicken apart and serve it with the cooking juices alongside anything from steamed rice and stir-fried vegetables to French bread and a salad. *Serves 4 to 6.*

Tip

A great way to peel a whole bunch of garlic is break up the head into cloves. Put these in a microwave-safe bowl and microwave on high for around 15 to 30 seconds, or until you begin to hear popping sounds from the garlic. Remove the bowl and wait a minute or two for the garlic to cool, and then slip the garlic cloves out of their sheaths.

Elder Paternal Aunt's Red-Cooked Pork

BÓMŬ DE HÓNGSHĀORÒU 伯母的紅燒肉

This is one of the few dishes Elder Paternal Aunt mastered, and I have to admit that it is delicious. Not only that, but with all those vegetables stretching out the meat, it's a meal that seems designed to keep the wolf from the door.

As far as my husband is concerned, her recipe is pure home cooking, and so I am never allowed to deviate from it by one iota.

12 dried black mushrooms
1 pound | 500 g pork belly
¼ cup | 35 g thinly sliced ginger
1 green onion, coarsely chopped
3 star anise
½ cup | 125 ml mild rice wine
2 cups | 500 ml boiling water, plus more as needed
1 tablespoon | 12 g rock sugar
2½ tablespoons regular Chinese soy sauce
1½ pounds | 700 g Yukon Gold potatoes

The night before you make this dish, place the dried mushrooms in a medium bowl and cover with cool water. The next day, snip off the stems and use those for something else. Cut the mushroom caps in half. Decant the soaking liquid into another bowl and discard the sediment.

Slice the pork into (more or less) 1-inch | 2-cm cubes and pat dry with a paper towel. Set a wok over medium heat, and when the bottom is hot, carefully set the pork cubes on the hot iron without adding any extra oil. They should begin to sizzle but not burn, so adjust the heat as needed. Brown the pork on all sides. Add the ginger about halfway through, and when the pork is caramelized all over, add the green onions and rice wine. Bring this to a boil and then add the mushroom soaking liquid, boiling water, and rock sugar. Lightly cover the wok and turn the heat down as low as you can get it, and slowly braise the pork for about 3 hours, adding more boiling water as needed to bring the liquid up to the original level.

After 3 hours, the pork should be very tender, so from now on shake the wok instead of stirring it around. Drizzle in the soy sauce. Cut the potatoes into (more or less) 1-inch | 2-cm chunks and add them to the wok. Gently shake the wok to scoot things around and add more boiling water if necessary. Lightly cover the wok, bring the liquid to a full boil, and then turn the heat back down to low. Slowly simmer the potatoes and pork until the potatoes are cooked through, about 30 to 40 minutes. Taste and adjust the seasoning. You can remove most of the fat at this point if you like (I don't, but see the Tips for directions on how to do this). Then raise the heat to high in order to quickly boil down the sauce until it is slightly syrupy.

Serve hot with steamed rice or steamed bread, as well as a vegetable or two. *Serves 4 as part of a multicourse meal.*

Tips

Other cuts of pork will work as long as they are well-streaked with fat, since this ensures tenderness at the end of a long braise. Belly with the skin attached is certainly nice, for the skin's collagen will lend a wonderful stickiness to the sauce; just be sure to use a spatter screen when you fry the skin, because it tends to bubble and spit as it fries.

Chicken and beef are delicious when cooked this way, too. As always, aim for fatty cuts, since this ensures tenderness, which means that chicken thighs and brisket will be perfect here. Braise any alternative meats only until they are tender.

You can turn this into a more elegant dish by leaving out the potatoes, and you can leave out the mushrooms if none are handy.

If you would prefer to remove the melted fat, simply drain the sauce into a wide bowl so that it cools quickly. Add a handful of ice cubes and gently swish the sauce around so that the fat solidifies. Remove the solid fat and remaining ice cubes with a slotted spoon and discard. Return the defatted sauce to the wok, bring everything to a simmer again, and then serve.

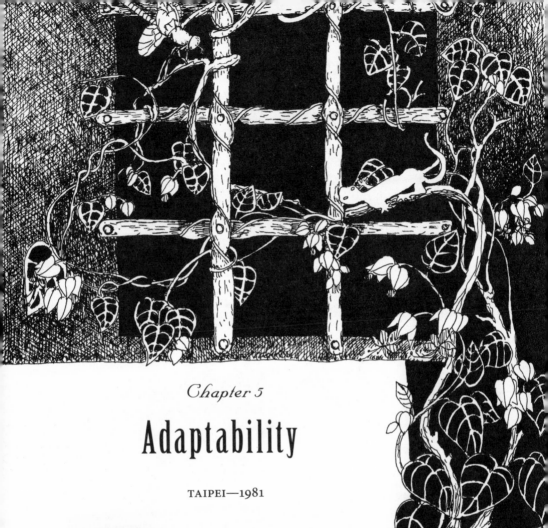

Chapter 5

Adaptability

TAIPEI—1981

More domesticated at this point than I ever thought possible, I am now officially a chatelaine in my off hours. I put together all of our curtains and pillow covers with a borrowed treadle sewing machine, and now our suburban townhouse in northern Taipei glows with the brilliant reds, blues, pinks, and greens

of the Hakkanese floral cotton fabric normally reserved for swad-
dling infants to the backs of farmers' wives.

We've hung old woodblock prints of Chinese deities on the walls,
and houseplants tangle their way up the windows. Our local friends
find all of this bizarre and amusing, as much as I would do if I found
them covering their sofas with lace and their pillows with corduroy.
Upstairs are the bedrooms and a bath, as well as a tiny balcony with
room for only two things: the little water heater and our laundry. The
bottom of our third-hand washing machine rusted out ages ago, but
it is propped up on found bricks to keep it more or less horizontal. It
thrashes our clothes in cold water and granular soap before spinning

them dry with a wall-shaking
roar, and then we hang our
shirts and pants on bamboo
poles suspended from the
veranda's ceiling. As decrepit
as this machine is, I will still
manage to find a buyer for it
four years down the line, since
washing machines remain a
luxury.

The single porch light in the
back attracts bevies of flying
insects, including shiny cock-
roaches enormous enough to
be windup toys, so we flick the
switch only when absolutely
necessary. Because we don't

have gas lines yet, we have to dial open a propane tank and turn on the heater just before we plan to bathe. It's considered terribly wasteful to keep even a pilot light burning, a fact that was drilled into me by my host family the first week I lived in Taipei. Leaving the water heater on after my shower was grounds for yet another serious discussion at the dining room table. I'd hang my head and make my apologies but usually forget sometime during the following week, and then we'd be back at the dining table for another heart-to-heart. That was five years past, a fifth of my life ago, and yet it feels like ancient history.

I FIND ENDLESS entertainment in all the little dramas unfolding behind the house. Ours is an extremely slender backyard, so I've trained staghorn and maidenhair and any other ferns I can find to grow on slabs of bark to create a vertical garden that decorates our cool, shaded, concrete wall. Because few of our neighbors bother with the areas around their houses—preferring to use them for storage or home factories more than anything else—the local wildlife flocks to our place in droves, setting up homes and staking claims among the plants.

A lizard hides in the fronds in wait for bugs to stumble by. A spider weaves a web that refracts the sunlight in its dewdrops. A delusional pale gecko hangs upside-down above the door and stalks a dragonfly twice its size, its long tail whipping around in excited snaps. Massive Mr. Toad looks more like a rock than an amphibian, and he reigns uncontested over this bit of wild acreage—our interactions consisting mainly of me saying hello to him and then using my broom to firmly shunt him into a reluctant hop so that I can sweep up all the cockroach mummies he has left behind in his wake. A solitary bat clings under a board propped against the back wall during the day, and geckos run in and out of the house at all hours in pursuit of a quick meal.

The first month here, I planted a discarded little duranta bush in our handkerchief of a front yard and then forgot about it until the roots reached the septic tank, which gave the twig all the encouragement it needed to erupt into a two-story tree that now shades the front bedroom. Throughout the summer, its frilly lavender blossoms hover in thick clusters like lilacs, their shade turning the cement underneath into a mossy carpet. By fall, the branches will bend toward the earth from their heavy amber constellations of tiny berries, which is why it is called the *golden dew flower* in Chinese.

Glorybower vines clamber up the front windows, their emerald leaves interspersed with flaming scarlet blossoms set inside the puffy white calyxes, a plant some fanciful Chinese person long ago christened *dragons spitting pearls*. Swordtail crickets trill like miniature carillons down the alley, informing us the exact day when the lunar season of Startled Insects has appeared in midspring. They are known locally as *little golden bells*, while our geckos are called *wall tigers*. The Chinese really have us beat at the naming game.

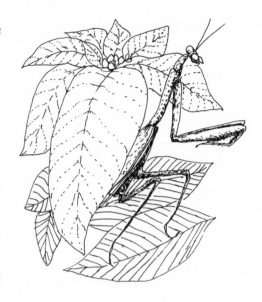

While the morning's mists still cling to the plants, I sweep up leaves in the front yard with a bamboo broom. Then, just before going back inside, I tap on the tree trunk to send a fresh shower of those lavender blossoms onto the moss. A ten-foot-tall poinsettia provides shelter for a single praying mantis that sedately weaves its upper body on its perch as if it were an ancient tai chi master. Black crickets hunker beneath our sofa during the cold winter nights and chirrup us to sleep. We leave those be, for J. H. tells me that they are the same little poetic emissaries as were described in the ancient *Book of Songs,* and that they will bring us good luck. We have a small shrine to the Earth God in the house, but I know that these creatures are the ones who truly watch over us.

Our home lies in the district called New Beitou. This is the prim suburban younger sister of Old Beitou, a resort town just to our east, where ladies of the evening still entertain both local and Japanese businessmen. This entrenched bit of sin is a holdover from Taiwan's half-century as an imperial colony, an era that ended only a little over thirty years ago. Nestled at the foot of Datun Mountain,

Old Beitou is covered with hot springs, its narrow gash of a valley befittingly sultry and often napped with mist. Raunchy hotels and resorts line both sides of the park that meanders up the valley and into the surrounding foothills. From there, hiking trails dogleg around thickets and temples, the endless green of the forest vibrating with talkative insects.

This can be mesmerizing, yet the occasional venomous snake keeps visitors from sinking too far under its spell. These are the offspring of a serpent stockpile the Japanese kept in a research facility on nearby Yangming Mountain and then released in a fit of deadly spite at being kicked out of Taiwan. I've learned whenever I'm skidding down a muddy trail not to reach out for a branch to slow my descent, as one time I almost grabbed a green bamboo viper by mistake and was saved only when my boyfriend yelled so loudly my ears rang for an hour. And yet it would be a shame not to venture there as often as possible, for white ginger flowers grow in the rainy valleys and brilliant birds sing from the treetops, their tropical plumage more like blossoms than feathers.

From the very beginning, I was confused by the name *Beitou*, because it doesn't mean anything in particular (literally, northern throw). However, one resource tells me that Beitou is the approximation of an indigenous word for *witch*, and that, on the other hand, makes complete sense, for this place is nothing less than enchanted. An iris farm lies only a few blocks from our home, its sea of paddies filled every year with cobalt blossoms undulating in the breeze. In early spring, before the bulbs have awakened, these flooded pools reflect the first bits of azure sky that follow our gray winters. By late spring, when the flowers are in full bloom, we pack a picnic lunch and seek out the clouds of snowy egrets that rise as one when startled, their shadows turning the irises many shades of purple.

We hike the foothills behind our home most weekends if we have time and the weather is good, and often clamber for hours over Datun Mountain to the village of Tamsui at the mouth of Taipei's river. Our goal is lunch, pure and simple. And for this we always

gravitate to Hundred Leaves Wenzhou Wontons. The owner, Mr. Ye, is from Ningbo, across the Taiwan Strait in coastal Zhejiang Province. His pork soup wontons are enclosed in wrappers as thin and white as silk, and they float in a simple broth topped with ribbons of yellow omelet and seaweed laver. Those eggy sponges contrast subtly with the wisps of fresh pasta, while the seaweed dissolves into a slurry that coats each mouthful.

The meal doesn't end there, though. Mr. Ye's icy-cold soy milk and crunchy roasted chicken legs are the perfect rewards for that long hike. The bird always arrives practically smoking from the hot oven, freshly whacked into convenient slices and sprinkled with rounds of green onions. Before taking a first bite, we reach for the Taiwan Beer bottle that Mr. Ye places on our table, for it is filled with homemade black vinegar, a friend's creation from Taiwan's northern port of Keelung. Rich and thick and sweet, this traditional recipe is Zhejiang Province's answer to Modena's glorious balsamic vinegar. Nothing at all like the weak, sour liquids marketed nowadays as Zhenjiang vinegar, this sticky elixir rightfully achieved culinary immortality many centuries ago. Mr. Ye meticulously peaks the bottle cap open so that the vinegar dribbles out easily. We saturate the chicken with this divinely simple sauce.

Sated and exhausted, J. H. and I stumble onto the bus and nap the whole way back.

FOR THE FIRST TIME that I can remember, I am completely happy. My boyfriend and I are at peace with each other and ourselves. Part of this is because we both have steady work—he's still an educator, while I'm juggling close to a dozen jobs—so money is finally not an issue.

More important to our happiness is simply that, aside from our normal share of disagreements, we usually have so little to fight about anymore. Our initial years together were tumultuous at times, but now the calm we feel around each other is startlingly comforting, the silence almost deafening. We are evolving, growing, maturing, and softening. The scars from our youths fade away as we insulate ourselves far from all the family kerfuffles on the other side of the Pacific. Few Americans interact with us anymore, so we mainly speak Mandarin at home. My jobs at the National Museum of History, National Central Library, National Museum of Natural Science, Academia Sinica, National Institute for Compilation and Translation, a couple of magazines, and assorted book-translation projects require that I speak English only rarely, and even then for very short periods of time. Because of this, I am shuffling off my Americanisms, my Western body language, and much of my foreign accent as I attempt to fit into this homogeneous society. Unless they are strangers, the people here are coming to treat me as they would anybody else, mainly because I'm assuming the colorations of my surroundings, like a moth on tree bark or an octopus disappearing into a coral reef.

As an official part of our neighborhood, I can look forward to being scolded by the local shopkeepers and regular hawkers if I am absent for more than a few days in a row. My favorite vendor around here is old Mr. Liu, a gentleman who rides his rusty bike past our house every morning at about breakfast time and announces his presence by calling out "*Bāozi mántóu!*" He practically sings his wares, starting out deep and slow before ascending the scale until the last syllable is stretched out into a rising cry, one that ends on a whiplash note sounding a whole lot like "whoa!" He always taps on his squeaky brakes as he approaches our gate, just to make sure I've heard him coming. Strapped over his rear tire is a large wooden box, which in turn encloses a padded blanket of white muslin to keep his northern-style steamed breads—the ones that enclose a filling (*bāozi*) and the ones that don't (*mántóu*)—hot and moist. These buns are chewy and fragrant from the levain he relies on to raise his homemade dough, for his is a one-man operation. Like so many of the older Mainland men here, he was part of the Nationalist Army that retreated to Taiwan in 1949. Good humor and an aching loneliness are etched in his beautifully lined face.

I wave him down one morning, pocket change at the ready to buy breakfast. "*Tàitài!*" he exclaims loudly in his heavy Shandong accent, for like all the other hawkers and shopkeepers I frequent, he courteously calls me *Ma'am*, even though I'm young enough to be his granddaughter. He brakes to a screeching halt in front of our gate and dismounts. "Where were you all last week? It's been forever! I thought you were mad at me."

"How could I ever be angry with you?" I ask. "I just had to leave for work early those days for a big exhibition at the museum. I'm sorry I missed you."

Nodding and satisfied that we are still on good terms, he moves over to the box. "What will it be today? Plain steamed *mántóu*, or my brown sugar ones? Pork-filled *bāozi,* or the ones with red bean paste?"

"Four brown sugar buns and two red bean buns, please." He tosses these into plastic bags before twirling them shut. "I threw in a couple of my pork buns just because you're my favorite customer." I laugh and tell him not to tease me.

"I mean it," he says. "Don't disappear on me again. I worry." When it comes to guilt trips, no mother in the world can hold a candle to the finely honed skills of my Chinese bun-seller.

DURING THESE PAST few years, my food vendors have often morphed into friends and teachers. This all started back when we rented an apartment in the Shipai District in 1980. My most beloved shopkeeper by far was Mr. Cong, the greengrocer, for he submitted with infinite patience to my questions about what was good and why and what something was called and how to cook it. We referred to him as "The Pope" because he always raised his hands in a papal-like blessing when I said good-bye. He, on the other hand, humored me as a relatively dim student of vegetables. I'd pick up a large Chinese radish, say, and start to put it in my pile, watching him out of the corner of my eye. A small crease between his brows would stop my hand in midair.

"Why isn't this one good?" I asked. "I felt it all over. It's hard, the tiny roots are not shriveled, and there are no bruises or bug holes. It feels heavy for its size. What am I missing?"

Mr. Cong smiled and crooked his forefinger at me, signaling me to bring it over. "Look at the base of the leaves. It's too old. It will be hot rather than juicy, hollow rather than solid."

"How can you tell it's old?"

"Look at the base of the leaves, I said. Look how wide it is. Look at all of those leaves. Those took a long time to grow, *Tàitài*. It has been in the soil too long." He picked up another one that appeared almost identical except for those leaves. "But see this one here—you only have a few leaves, a very small bunch of them. This one is young, and it grew fast. You want this one." With a satisfied nod, he put it aside for me. And then he showed me a pile of something else to study: bamboo shoots.

"Tell me which ones are good and which ones will be bitter, which ones are fresh and which ones are not." He always wore a grin as he played this game, for I think he enjoyed it as much as I did. I recalled our previous lessons as I pawed through his hillock of brownish cones, squeezing them toward the tips to ensure they were solid and not dried out, holding them up to my nose to locate the proper aroma of damp earth and morning dew, and running my thumbs across the bases to certify that the ends were freshly cut and not yet scabbing over. I triumphantly set a few in front of him.

Mr. Cong chuckled. "You have two sweet ones and seven bitter ones. Which two look different from the others?" I felt like an idiot in front of the other ladies shopping away, getting quizzed out there in the open, but I tried not to let it show. Besides, the other shoppers were listening intently to what he had to say and auditing my vegetable class, as it were.

"Uh," I said, after fussing around with the shoots, trying to find what set them apart, "these two have yellow tips? And the others are green?"

"Exactly!" And then he looked at me very seriously. "Now tell me, why would yellow tips tell you they are sweet and green ones tell you they are bitter?" The ladies whipped their heads around to stare at me, willing me to answer. I suddenly remembered something about photosynthesis, chlorophyll, and all the other stuff that had wandered into my brain some time during seventh-grade science class. I didn't have a clue how to say photosynthesis or chlorophyll in Chinese. This called for made-up language and lots of signage.

"The bamboo shoots are, uh, underground, and don't see the sun. Uh, they're still storing sugar in the plant, yes?" I got an encouraging nod from the teacher. "The shoot comes up out of the ground, sees the sun, starts to grow, turns green, and the sugar, um, pfft? Goes away?"

Mr. Cong practically patted me on the head. Nods all around as the ladies murmured something about photosynthesis and chlorophyll in Chinese. And I wondered how Mr. Cong was ever going to be able to unload his bitter bamboo shoots now that the cat was out of the bag.

Longan Tea with Fresh Ginger (V)

LÓNGYǍN JIĀNG CHÁ 龍眼薑茶 OR
GUÌYUÁN JIĀNG CHÁ 桂圓薑茶

One of the biggest perks of working at the National Museum of History was teatime with my many friends there. No matter the weather, we would try to carve out time for gossip over afternoon refreshments in any one of the beautiful teahouses we frequented. Most of the time, we would spring for the freshest oolong teas on the menu and revel in their floral perfumes. But we all agreed that after slogging our way through the alleyways in the rain on cold winter days, nothing satisfied the soul like this delicate sweet soup. Called a "tea" in Chinese because it is a clear broth, this simple yet glorious concoction tastes of smoke and fruit and spice.

1 cup | 100 g (or so) peeled and pitted dried longans
8 cups | 2 liters water
1 tablespoon finely shredded peeled ginger
Brown sugar, agave syrup, or honey to taste (optional)

Rinse the longans in a sieve under cold water and place them in a medium saucepan. Cover them with the water and bring to a full boil. Reduce the heat to low, add the ginger, and slowly simmer the longans for about 30 minutes, or until the fruits are pale and plump.

Taste and add some sweetener, if you like. You may strain out the fruit or leave it in. Serve hot. You can make this ahead and store it in the fridge for a couple of days before reheating and serving—as with almost all soups, it will taste even better that way. *Serves about 8.*

Tip

A fresh longan looks a bit like a small lychee, as the thin tan shell covers a layer of fragrant white flesh that in turn envelops a large brown pit. But this recipe calls for dried ones, which are sold already shelled and pitted. These tropical fruits resemble large amber raisins at this point, and they possess a deep, sweet perfume. For more information, see page 269 in the Glossary and Basic Recipes.

Simple Radish Soup (V)

LUÓBO QĪNGTĀNG 蘿蔔清湯

Mr. Cong would have advised me to reserve this recipe for cool weather, when big Asian radishes are sweet rather than hot, juicy rather than woody. These raw vegetables—especially Korean *mooli* radishes—then taste like the most heavenly of apples, so you can just peel, slice, and eat. Most other Asian radishes work well here, too, including Chinese *luóbo* and Japanese daikon.

This is the sort of soup that I serve when something fatty is on the menu—roast duck from a favorite deli, say, or stir-fried sausages with pickles—because it offers nothing but a gentle sweetness. If we're having guests, I'll julienne the radishes into fine threads, which gives them a silky texture that belies the austerity of this palate-cleansing soup. Don't worry too much about measurements here, for this is definitely a recipe where you can wing it.

1 Asian radish (about 1 pound | 500 g) of any kind
Water, as needed

Remove the skin of the radish with a potato peeler. If you see tough webbing under the skin, remove that too. Cut off the ends and then slice the radish into batons or fine julienne. Place in a saucepan and cover with about 1 inch | 2 cm of water. Simmer uncovered until the radish is tender. That's it. No salt, no oil, no ginger. It's really that perfect. *Serves 4.*

Chapter 6

Consistency

TAIPEI—1982

C lose your eyes and taste this."

I hear him uncover the dish, and the clicking of chopsticks suggests he is searching around for the perfect morsel to feed me. Tingling heat from fresh ginger and the aroma of green onions rise up to my nose. My lips open in anticipation. As I gently bite into the thin slip of meat he has placed in my mouth, I marvel at an unidentifiable core flavor wrapped in caramel, star anise, and rich soy sauce. This strange flesh tastes a bit like fish, and it is no land animal, that's for sure.

I chew and swallow, but I have no idea what that was. "*Zàilái yīkuài*," I say, demanding another piece from my dining companion, and a ribbon of green onion slithers over my tongue in response, ushering in a shred of meat and skin that challenges me to speak its name. My fingers hunt around on the table for my teacup. I take a sip, clear my palate, and ask for a hint.

"We call it 'the skirt edge,'" he explains very unhelpfully in Chinese. "Now open wide. This is going to be a bigger piece with some hard bits, so chew carefully."

My teeth close down warily on something solid like a crab's carapace, but it is too thick for that, plus the flavor is most decidedly not crustacean. More slippery skin encases its exterior, while inside huddles that unmistakable suggestion of fish/not fish. Shaoxing rice wine's luscious sherry and mushroom overtones have insinuated themselves into every corner of this chunk, and my tongue works in concert with my lips to seek out more of these flavors as I suck it clean. After removing the shell with my own chopsticks, I play with it on my plate, keeping my eyes closed as promised. Not a clue.

"*Hǎoba*," my tormentor says, taking slight pity on me with the Chinese version of "okay." He changes tactics and sets a soft sphere against my lips. "*Zhè shì shénmo?*" Mealy and slightly wrinkled, the orb surrenders easily to my molars as an earthy sweetness fills my mouth. Smokiness sidles up my nose as it heads its way down to my stomach.

"Dried chestnut?" I murmur in Mandarin. The only sign he gives to indicate whether I'm correct is that I get to breathe in the slippery little egg set against my lips. A whole garlic clove—one that was peeled and then gently cooked into submission—puddles on my tongue. Another kind of sweetness is released, though admittedly more than a bit rowdy after that demure chestnut.

I am on one of my regular dinner dates with J. H. We are feasting at our favorite haunt, a quiet restaurant in downtown Taipei that specializes in classic dishes from Zhejiang and Jiangsu, the provinces that surround Shanghai and serve as that massive city's main culinary influences. The chef and servers have come to know us quite well. We only have to walk in the door to have our favorite appetizers set in front of us, and then we are informed of the day's specials and the chef's recommendations.

Mealy braised favas almost always appear alongside our cups of hot green tea. Their barely sprouted roots tell us that the starch of the dried beans has been awakened and turned ever so slightly vegetal. These olive-hued purses are culinary teases that require the diner to slow down, work the seasoned insides out one by one through oral calisthenics involving adept tongues and teeth, and then gracefully discard the leathery exteriors via chopsticks.

At other times, when the chef is in an especially good mood, peeled favas might be turned into a sort of pâté replete with finely minced country ham and pickles. Or, if the weather is

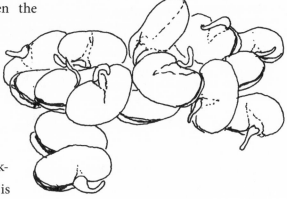

hot, we can look forward to a cool plate of crunchy jellyfish heads—which is what the Chinese call the cauliflower-like blossoms underneath the creature's smooth cap—that have been dried and salted and then blanched before being tossed with fragrant black Zhenjiang-style vinegar and a handful of aromatic vegetables in order to rouse our hunger.

The waitress smiles in my direction as she sets down another appetizer, one she knows is especially for me, one that I don't even have to bother ordering anymore: two raw, black, preserved eggs perched on a tumble of tender, blanched bean curd. Other customers get only one jellylike egg, but I prefer the creaminess of two, so now an extra one always gets slipped in silently as a special gift. These have been exactingly sliced into thin wedges, their velvety centers oozing out over the quivering little cubes of doufu and their wobbly exteriors fading to gray where they angle toward points, as this creation is an homage to the various degrees of softness one can find in the simplest ingredients. Just before serving this dish, the chef quickly heats a smattering of aromatics in oil and a splash of soy sauce—necessary savory adjuncts to those intensely bland yet creamy ingredients—and splashes it over the top. Tiny specks of pickles sparkle on our taste buds with each bite. We eat this by the glorious spoonful, the one appetizer that allows us to wallow in it with abandon while our stomachs growl in anticipation.

All of these appetizers have been created as silent requests for our undivided attention. They set the mood for leisurely meals that at first tease the senses and then very gradually sate our appetites. No instant gratification is ever offered. Instead, we must settle back and acquiesce, leaving the world behind. The purring gourmet sitting across from me is teaching me the delights that can arise out of yielding the reins to someone more knowledgeable, be it an older lover or a chef. And today he is setting the stage for both of us to be transported into the proper mental state required to truly appreciate a great meal, one that will open us up to this particular master's gifts and help us comprehend his lifetime of experience, as well as the teachings of all the chefs who went before him.

A favorite appetizer here is called Suzhou-style smoked fish. But in China's classic cuisines, part of the fun of dining is that things are not always as they seem, or as advertised. Magic has been a common denominator in all of the most exquisite Chinese meals I've ever eaten, either through disguising the true nature of the main ingredient—and thus creating a surprising gap between what the eyes perceive and what the tongue decides is real—or by intimating one thing while delivering another.

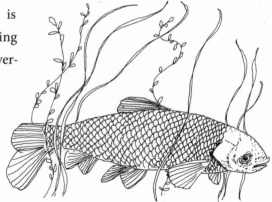

For example, in this dish the fish is not really smoked, it just looks like it. The preparation is deceptively simple: Thick chunks of marinated carp are deep-fried without batter until crisp and golden, and then a touch of moisture is returned via a rich braise, a step that supplies an enticing chewiness to the flesh. The strong bones are left in to keep the fish from falling apart. These also act as gentle suggestions to pace ourselves and to feel each morsel as it works its way across our mouths, so that we may contemplate the life of this particular animal. Shaoxing rice wine and braised green onions release and then tame the subtly muddy flavors of the flesh, reminding us that this carp once lived in a freshwater lake and fed on creatures hidden in the silt down below the filtered sunlight. It therefore becomes more than an anonymous chunk of fish to be wolfed down without a thought, and instead offers up sensory echoes from the carp's brief sojourn on this planet. It enters into our bodies and becomes part of us, and we are encouraged to honor the gifts of its existence and of its death.

THE FOOD AT this restaurant, known as Fuxingyuan, is uniformly excellent and absolutely faithful to the time-honored recipes of East China. Nestled at the confluence of many waterways, great and small, this area is also home to some of the best food in the world. Upriver from here is Chinese wine country, and so, much as in places like Dijon and Northern California, rich and savory dishes have been designed to complement and even magnify the local wines. But, unlike in the West, China's wines are coaxed out of vats of sticky rice rather than grapes. Once upon a time, and up to almost the exact middle of the twentieth century, the amber brews of Shaoxing had been every bit as storied and finessed as the products of the Loire, at least as far as Chinese connoisseurs were concerned. And, just as with any good French or California wine, these have traditionally been created in a glorious spectrum of light and mild to heavy and sweet, albeit with delectable suggestions of summer's warmth or a bouquet of fresh mushrooms or even honey-scented flowers.

During the first few decades of twentieth century, the modern city of Shanghai came to strut an imperial eclecticism in its foods in a way that would have made old Vienna sigh with envy. Touches of the grand gastronomic capitals of Chengdu to the west, Beijing to the north, and Guangzhou to the south wound their way into this dish and that with extraordinary flair, but the main influences remained, as always, the great food centers upstream on the Chang Jiang (which means the Long River but is mistakenly known in English as the Yangtze)* and its myriad tributaries. The result is that many traditional Shanghainese creations celebrate the best ingredients money can buy.

---

* The third-longest river in the world, the Chang Jiang starts in the Tibetan Plateau and empties into the East China Sea almost four thousand miles later. Chinese people

One of our favorites at this restaurant, especially during the coldest months, is *yānduxiān*, or Shanghai sandpot. Served in the rough pottery casserole that gives the dish its English name, this is a rich *pot-au-feu* teeming with ginger, Shaoxing rice wine, ham or salt pork, fresh pork belly, fat bamboo shoots, black mushrooms, and bean curd knots. Those two kinds of pork conspire to create a subtle alchemy, but most of their rendered fat is removed, as it would otherwise muffle the dance of flavors. Bean curd knots—thin layers of compressed doufu looped into a simple tie—serve as squeaky, ingenious sponges that squirt the flavors of the other ingredients across teeth and tongues with each bite.

Another dish we order often during the cold months is red-cooked lion heads—*red-cooked* meaning that soy sauce and rock sugar are combined to shade the sauce a rich mahogany. Lion heads are usually described as meatballs, but the ones in this restaurant are airy rather than meaty, and finely chopped fresh water chestnuts spangle the interior, waking up the palate with delicate traces of crunch and sweetness. Some say

—————
often find it amusing that we call the entire river the Yangtze, for this name refers only to the section between Nanjing and Shanghai.

they are called lion heads because these softball-size orbs sit in a tangle of napa cabbage that might have reminded someone of the big cats'
manes. But since they don't look like any lion I've ever seen, I attribute
this strange name to another one of life's mysteries. Lions turn into
pussycats, though, whenever our chef slides translucent, silky sheets
made out of mung bean starch into the bottom of the sandpot. Called
fěnpí, they look like plastic in their dry state but turn fat and slippery
as they soak up the rich broth. When done right, *fěnpí* slithers across
the lips and tongue in an almost lascivious way. It's sex in a casserole.

Over time, senses must have been overwhelmed and appetites jaded
by all this opulence, which is why East China's great chefs rely on wit
as a way of counteracting boredom in their dedicated diners. A bowl
of something called fish noodle soup will therefore
turn me rapturous when I find that it literally consists of puffy strands of finely ground freshwater
fish swimming in a clear stock scented with a touch
of pale rice vinegar. Light and airy, these noodles
vanish on my tongue and leave behind just a suggestion of the animal, as if it had somehow swum
past my nose and disappeared behind my ears.

In the hands of a really clever chef, reality tends
more often than not to be impishly tweaked, while
presumptions are dashed with the
charm and deftness of a conjurer.
The first time I noticed this was
at a fancy Hunanese restaurant
where the table was graced with a
beautiful porcelain tureen, its interior

and exterior fully decorated with the sort of rampant *famille rose* design that would definitely be more at home in a palace than a restaurant. A fluffy mound of cilantro and toasted rounds of fried crullers crouched at the bottom of the bowl, and that was it. I was confused, as I had thought I'd heard that we were going to finish the meal with a fish soup. A waitress walked up to our table carrying a large steel kettle that vibrated with heat. She politely gestured to us to lean back and then poured the hot stock into the tureen with a practiced, circular flourish. White petals magically appeared on the surface as translucent shards of carp were swept off the tureen's interior by the steaming current and instantly blanched. She ladled out a small bowl for me. The barely cooked fish melted on my tongue, while the crispy crullers and sprightly cilantro offered gentle counterpoints of texture, flavor, and color. It was then that I understood the need for all that fancy decoration on the porcelain, because it had allowed the raw slices to cling stealthily to the inner wall. The soup was perfection, but that sleight-of-hand was what truly bewitched me.

It doesn't end there. In other restaurants, soy skins are filled with seasoned minced pork and deep fried in order to pretend that they had somehow been transformed into what are then called chicken rolls. Ersatz crab is a clever transformation of everyday chicken eggs into something that looks and tastes and smells like the shelled crustacean. And one of my favorites has always been winter melon prepared to look like a square of red-cooked pork. It is such a flawless impersonation that I have successfully fooled vegetarians into thinking I was trying to make them eat meat for dinner. The skin is crosshatched, fried to golden brown, and then deeply stained with

the caramelized sauce. I don't
know the science behind
it, but these colors seep
into the melon's flesh
in perfect layers so that
you end up with striations of
mahogany and beige, just like a
slab of braised pork belly.

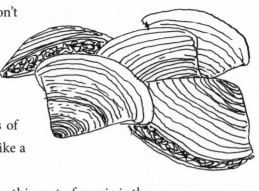

The enchanted vortex for this sort of magic is the
fertile Yangtze River Delta, where you might be served a platter of
fresh clams, their shells shiny and wet. They swim in a translucent
sauce, their ribbed gray shells darkening as they coalesce toward
the hinges. You see specks of coral peeking out of the edges and
think, "Ahhh, that old cliché, stuffed clams." But when you pluck
one up with your chopsticks, a slight give in the shell comes across
as distinctly disturbing. You clench the clam even more firmly with
your chopsticks, intrigued and yet suddenly anxious that this slippery morsel might shoot out across the table. Cradling it with a soup
spoon, you carry it up to your mouth, still unsure of what you are
about to eat. It smells divinely of the wetlands and of wine and ginger, but no other clues are forthcoming. You place it between your
lips, and a first tentative bite informs you that the shell is in reality a tender slice of grass carp. Startled and confused, you exam-
ine it more closely. In front of you lies a triangle of butterflied fish
loin filled with shrimp forcemeat that has been steamed and then
napped with a sauce.

The mimicry is perfect. The result is stunning. The diner has been
fooled. And the diner is delighted.

And so, gastronomy in the eastern part of China is home to some of the most sensuous meals on the planet. In the right hands, every component seems to be designed to seduce the diner one way or the other. That is why a simple steamed fish might offer up little surprises like bits of cured ham sandwiched into its sides to season the flesh from within, while a thin netting of caul fat on the outside melts in the moist heat so that each bite is cossetted with a creamy undercurrent. Dried ingredients such as bonito and cuttlefish and shrimp lend earthy depth, meaty texture, and gentle salinity to slow-cooked casseroles, but only because they are perfectly poised against something bright and juicy, such as fresh chicken or pork or doufu. It's all about how opposites attract. Nuance is the byword, surprise the goal, and gratified sighs the reward.

J. H. soothingly prods my inchoate yearnings by sliding his favorite foods into my mouth, telling me to stop asking questions, to just listen to what my senses are saying. He gradually makes me desire ingredients that have no English names and combinations that he knows will bewilder me if I ever get to overanalyze them beforehand. I have thus turned into his protégée, his hobby, his entertainment, his constant dining companion. Plates are set before me in his wordless challenge to embrace this otherworldly sensuality. And tonight, as we do many times a week, we play our game.

My teacher searches out dishes that will instruct, that will feed my mind even more than my appetite. Dinner becomes an array of minor wonders that reveal themselves only when subjected to intense scrutiny by all my senses. Curls of dried fish swim bladder hide ninja-like in a tumble of fresh shrimp, their pale bubbles offering a peculiarly tensile resistance against those pink commas of crisp crustacean—or at least they seem peculiar until I realize that because of them I must slowly consume each mouthful while the white sponges begrudgingly release a froth of flavors onto my tastebuds, amplifying in turn the sweetness of the shrimp. My molars tread gingerly nowadays over strange objects as my tongue tries to parse out hidden identities, to match Chinese names to the Chinese ingredients, to figure out the reality that is posing as mere supper.

And, of all things, I've come to like sea cucumbers. In Shanghainese restaurants like this one, these odd beasts that look like massive slugs shuffling around in robes covered with soft spines soak up a thick glaze of flavors with a buttery finish through a long, slow wallow in a sauce seasoned by pork belly, chicken broth, soy sauce, rice wine, and rock sugar. At the end of a few hours, their gelatinous texture bounces softly in happy accord with unctuous porky clouds of fat, skin, and muscle. Once I had let my guard down on something that weird and beguiling, there was no turning back.

As WE DELVE deeper into his country's gastronomy, I am becoming more and more cognizant of how much the *yin* here requires a measured counterweight of the *yang*: hot against cold, soft against hard, animal against vegetable, dry against fresh, raw against cooked, savory against sweet, bland against spicy, plain against fancy, and fermented against salted. Smells and tastes have proved to me that they possess spectrums every bit as broad and vibrant as the rainbow. Consistencies reveal themselves as I eat, their vibrations echoing through my teeth and up into my brain. I revel in the tackiness of sticky rice batons or braised pork tendons when they pleasantly glue my molars together. I gently force them apart, creating a slight snap that ripples past the back of my eyes. The deep crunch of fried fish bones rebounds against my eardrums, while the smooth textures of chilled agar, bean jellies, and river eel glide down my throat like whispers. Chile peppers slip through my lips in endless permutations. Dried therapeutic herbs and roots and flowers rumble around on the brink of my cognizance, opening up synapses and reordering my comprehension of what could and should constitute culinary seasoning.

Fat beguiles me in ways I could not have anticipated. I was brought up to believe that fat—and especially animal fat—was bad. But over these past few months, I've begun to see that it satisfies my hunger, soothes my tongue, and reinterprets flavors. It acts as an unctuous conduit and mediator, a most necessary component in virtually every dish. I now greedily seek out those luxuriously silky yellow layers weaving under a bird's skin and down through its thighs, as well as the vibrant coral butter hidden inside crispy fried shrimp heads, a lava that leaks onto my palate like a sigh.

I work that bit of mystery meat around in my mouth for a few minutes more.

"Any more hints?"

"No. Come on, figure it out."

It seems like its name is tiptoeing on the edge of my mind, that I might have tasted it once before, but right now I don't know what it could possibly be. "Honestly, I give up." I sneak a peek at the dish in front of me. Dark brown chunks of that something-or-other are studded with those white garlic cloves and amber chestnuts. Turning my chopsticks upside-down so that only the fat, decorative tops touch the serving dish, I prod the deeply hued squares. I finally find one with an acute angle in the shell. An inch of that silky skin extends out from the corner, and it's slightly frilled.

"That's the skirt I was talking about," he smiles. I see a head poking out from under a green onion. Ah, it's terrapin, a freshwater turtle. Yes, land and water combined into one animal. I have eaten few amphibians other than the occasional frog leg before this evening, but now that I know what this is, the creature's essence practically shouts at me. Plucking up a particularly meaty piece, I place it on my mound of rice and then nestle another chestnut and garlic clove in there so that I can fill my mouth with all three ingredients. They combine on my palate like a symphony, the soy and turtle frolicking with everything in there that is sweet and savory and aromatic.

An hour later, we finish our meal and step outside. He takes my hand as we stroll toward our bus stop, the humid night air wafting sweet aromas from a nearby night market around our heads.

"Dessert?" I suggest. He beams and leads the way.

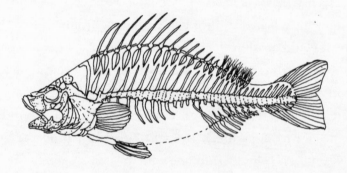

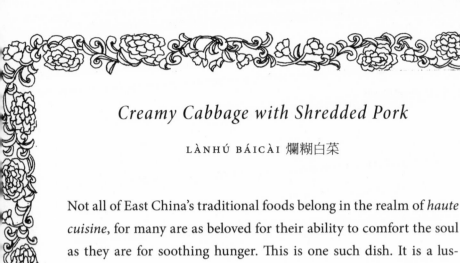

Creamy Cabbage with Shredded Pork

LÀNHÚ BÁICÀI 爛糊白菜

Not all of East China's traditional foods belong in the realm of *haute cuisine*, for many are as beloved for their ability to comfort the soul as they are for soothing hunger. This is one such dish. It is a luscious combination of super-tender cabbage threads seasoned with a bit of pork. While that might not sound like much, the result is incomparable.

I have changed up the recipe a bit by suggesting you toss the raw pork with pink curing salt—the same thing that's used in hams and salamis—to lend it more personality and turn it a pretty rosy hue, but it's also perfectly delicious without this extra ingredient.

Under no circumstances should you try to substitute heartier head cabbage for the delicate leaves of napa cabbage, for only the latter will predictably collapse into silky strands. To be perfectly honest, the amount of cabbage will probably terrify you as you slice it up, but I promise that it will cook down quickly into a sweet, porridge-like puddle with savory notes from the chicken stock and pork. This is heavenly.

PORK

About 2 ounces | 60 g lean boneless pork

½ teaspoon fine sea salt

A good pinch of pink curing salt (optional)

1 head napa cabbage (1 to 1½ pounds | 500 to 750 g)

3 tablespoons peanut or vegetable oil

1 tablespoon finely shredded peeled ginger

2 cups | 500 ml unsalted or low-sodium chicken stock

½ teaspoon sugar

¼ teaspoon fine sea salt, or to taste

Boiling water, as needed

2 teaspoons cornstarch, mixed with 2 tablespoons cool water

Place the pork in the freezer for about 30 minutes, as it will be much easier to slice if it's partially frozen. Cut the pork across the grain into thin slices, and then cut these into thin strips. Place the pork in a small bowl and toss with the fine sea salt and optional pink curing salt. Cover the bowl and refrigerate the pork for a couple of hours if you're using the pink curing salt; otherwise, 15 minutes will do if it's just the sea salt. Rinse the pork thoroughly in a colander and drain it on paper towels.

Clean and core the cabbage, then cut it against the grain into a thin julienne.

Place a wok over high heat and swirl in the oil once the wok is hot. Add the ginger and toast it quickly in the oil to release its fragrance. Sprinkle in the pork shreds and then toss the pork over the heat until it has turned pale. Scrape the pork and ginger into a clean bowl, leaving as much of the oil in the wok as possible.

Return the wok to high heat, add the cabbage, and toss until it has wilted. Stir in the pork, stock, sugar, and fine sea salt and bring the liquid to a boil. Reduce the heat to medium to maintain a gentle simmer and cook uncovered for about 20 minutes, until the cabbage is very tender, adding a bit of boiling water to the wok if the stock cooks away too quickly. Stir the cornstarch mixture again, drizzle it around the cabbage, and then mix it in thoroughly by swirling the wok around. When the sauce has thickened and turned glossy, taste and adjust the seasoning.

Scoop the cabbage onto a rimmed plate or into a bowl. All you need here for a comforting dinner is steamed rice. *Serves 4.*

Tip
This is a dish that is designed to celebrate the silky nature of napa cabbage, and so the pork shows up here as only a supporting character. If you would prefer something meatier, just double the pork, along with the sea salt and optional pink curing salt.

Chilled Winter Melon with Wine and Ginger (V)

JĬUXIĀNG LIÁNG DŌNGGUĀ 酒香涼冬瓜

Although I talk about dinners in fancier restaurants in this chapter, J. H. and I ate most of our East Chinese meals in cheaper joints. What these places lacked in low lighting and ambience, they more than made up for with affordable meals that managed to thrill. This particular appetizer was served in a charmless dining room in downtown Taipei, but it was one with a genius cook or two hidden away in the kitchen.

Like so many of my favorite things to eat, this doesn't promise much on the surface, for it's just winter melon steamed until soft and then soaked in a heady marinade seasoned mainly with ginger and Shaoxing rice wine. But it looks and tastes stunning. I have added lemon zest and juice for another layer of flavors, and I'm in love with the result. Make this the day before you plan to serve it.

A square piece of winter melon (about 1 pound | 500 g and as flat as possible)

2 teaspoons mushroom seasoning, plus more to taste

2 tablespoons Shaoxing rice wine, plus more to taste

1 tablespoon fresh ginger juice

1 lemon, preferably a Meyer lemon

2 tablespoons julienned young ginger

Rinse the winter melon and pat dry. Remove the seeds and membranes, then cut off any corners that stick up too much. Slash the flesh down the length of the melon into strips about 1 inch | 2 cm wide, cutting all the way down to, but not through, the skin. Turn the melon 90 degrees and slash the flesh again into strips about 1 inch | 2 cm wide.

Set up a steamer. Place the melon on a rimmed heatproof plate and sprinkle with the mushroom seasoning and rice wine. Set it in the steamer and steam until the flesh is tender, about 20 to 30 minutes. Remove from the heat.

When the melon has cooled enough to handle easily, put it flesh side down in a container and pour in any liquid from the plate. Taste the liquid, and add more mushroom seasoning and rice wine as needed. Pour in the ginger juice. Zest the lemon and sprinkle in the zest, then add about a teaspoon of lemon juice. Cover the container and refrigerate the melon overnight.

Just before serving, use a thin blade to cut the flesh loose from the skin without disrupting its natural shape, and discard the skin. Place the melon on a rimmed serving plate. Taste the sauce again and adjust the seasoning as needed. Sprinkle the julienned ginger over the melon and serve cold. *Serves 4 to 6 as an appetizer.*

Tip

If you are unable to purchase winter melons in your area, consider growing them, especially the smaller, volleyball-sized ones. Seeds are available online from a variety of sources; the Bay Area's Kitazawa Seed Co. is a favorite of mine for its lovely range of East Asian vegetable seeds, including garlic chives and Chinese eggplant. I've also had great luck with both Renee's Garden and Baker Creek Heirloom Seed Company. Do note that winter melon is sometimes labeled as wax gourd, ash gourd, or *dong gua*, depending upon the seller.

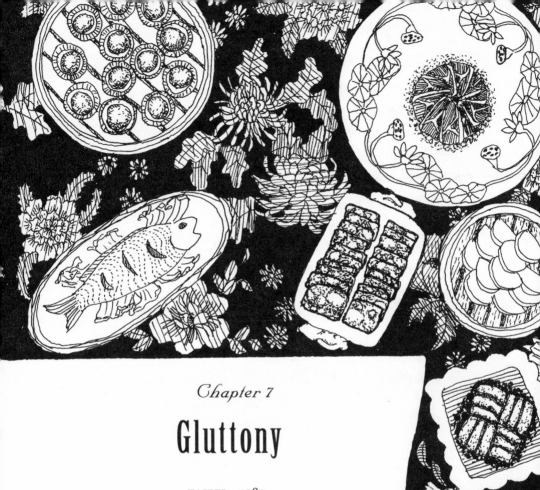

Chapter 7

Gluttony

TAIPEI—1983

At the best of all repasts, diners tend to be too enraptured by the food even to consider putting their thoughts into words. This evening I am sitting at just such a table with the director of the National Museum of History and his guest of honor. I am supposed to be working as the interpreter, but my mouth is way too full to talk.

Twelve of us are dining at one of Director Ho Hao-tien's favorites, Peng's Gourmet, a place that offers nothing but odes to Hunan's classic cuisines. Westerners know of Chef Peng Chang-kuei thanks to his most famous creation, General Tso's chicken.* As of yet, however, that's never, ever been served here. Instead, we are dining on the *ne plus ultra* of Changsha, Hunan's legendary culinary capital. Even though the inland province of Hunan is renowned for its searingly spicy dishes, barely a single chile pepper makes an appearance at a proper Hunanese feast like this. Much like in Chengdu, the banquet foods of Changsha accentuate subtle transformations in flavor, texture, and presentation as the meal progresses, while chiles are, for the most part, reserved for street foods and home-style dishes. So, the heaviest seasonings we generally are treated to at sybaritic celebrations like these are fermented black beans and cured meats pinged with ginger and garlic.

We start the dinner with a specialty of the house: smoked Hunan-style cured pork steamed until tender in a honey sauce scented with the tiny blossoms known as Osmanthus, or *guìhuā*, and then served in half-moons of steamed bread. The elderly American woman to my

---

* Legend has it that Chef Peng, who happened to cook for the generalissimo from time to time, created this in 1952 for Admiral Arthur W. Radford, commander of the United States Pacific Fleet, so the chef flatteringly named it after one of Hunan's most famous military commanders. However, since this was intended to please an American at a time when all of China's cuisines were thought to taste more or less like Chinese American dishes, General Tso's chicken turns out to be little more than sweet-and-sour chicken flecked with dried chiles.

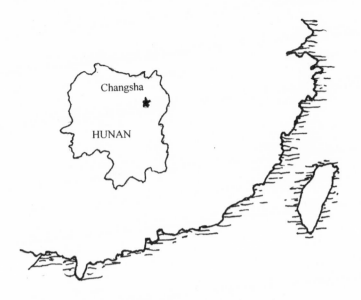

left just released a little moan as she bit into this, the world's best ham sandwich, and I can hardly blame her, for it is especially wonderful tonight, the perfect balance of smoke, salt, perfume, and sugar. I can even hear her molars come together as they hit the crispy surprise hidden inside: deep-fried doufu skins. Our guest is floored by this unexpected combination, this extravagant nod to textural layers, and another delighted whimper escapes her.

The chefs here are hitting their stride in the early 1980s, and Chinese-style restaurant dining has probably never been better. We revel in the moment as we spin the lazy susan, toasting each other with tea and dotingly slipping morsels onto our neighbors' plates in a hospitable game of manners—one that breaks the ice and sets us up for brief bouts of conversation between the courses. As the ham gradually disappears, we uncover braised fresh lotus seeds nestled in that complex sauce. There is a quiet pause while we admire how their gentle, almost vegetal mealiness contrasts with the caramelized syrup. Freshly harvested lotus seeds are an indulgence we are lucky to enjoy for only a few weeks in autumn, so the platter is picked clean just before something else arrives to astonish us.

I look forward to another of Chef Peng's creations with anxious anticipation, for it is one of my favorite final courses here: minced pigeon in bamboo cups. The waitress carries a heavy tray of bamboo cups directly from the steamer to our table, then carefully decants them into the porcelain soup bowls set before us. The squab barely manages to cling to an almost elusive solidity as it floats in the clear broth. This bit of legerdemain is created after the backs of two wide Chinese knives are called upon to whack raw squab meat and good pork together into a feathery paste. The chef then folds in chopped water chestnuts and a small handful of aromatics before whipping in lots of seasoned stock. This is poured into bamboo cups, where it is steamed to create cloudlike masses. We are already very full, but the resulting meatball is so light that it evaporates on the tongue, and we eagerly swallow the rich broth while it is still hot. Happy and sated at last, we sit back and enjoy the liquid heat first as it slowly courses its way down our bodies, and then as it soothes our distended bellies and caresses the remains of that magnificent meal.

When the stars are aligned correctly, a Chinese meal can feel like an adroit combination of sorcery and silliness. The first time this happened to me was when a waiter at Peng's Gourmet placed a small soup bowl at my place as the final savory course. I peered at what looked for all the world like a peeled hard-boiled egg, wondering why anyone would bother to offer up such a boring thing at such an otherwise finessed meal. Yes, I'll admit this unexciting egg was adorned with some black mushrooms and a bone broth, and perhaps a few leaves of blanched green bok choy swam around to brighten things up, yet I had for all intents and purposes been served lunchbox fare. But then it trembled when I touched it, a sub-tle hint that things were not as they appeared. Using my chopsticks, I nicked off a piece and slurped it up. The egg white melted on my tongue into a puddle of perfectly seasoned chicken stock, ginger, and wine. Intrigued, I pinched off a side of the egg, eager to find and taste the yolk. There was none. The whole thing was a fusion of albu-men and savoriness, a ridiculous yet tasty poke in the eye. I know you're not supposed to laugh at the dinner table, but sometimes you just can't help it. I felt nothing short of glee as I siphoned down the rest of the egg.

KŎUGĂN. It's such a Chinese concept, one that more or less refers to the texture in food—everything from the most refined imperial dishes to the gummy fat tapioca balls in pearl tea—but the direct translation of *kǒugǎn* into "mouthfeel" provides a much better description of what this is all about.

As an aristocratic old gentleman from Jiangsu Province's Huai Yang region once explained it to us over a leisurely dinner, "*Kǒugǎn* refers to the sensation of food on every part of the tongue and the way it caresses the lips. It's also there in the degree of resistance the jaws encounter." Our refined host dreamily worked his chin a little bit as he said that. He took a sip of tawny rice wine and meditated a few moments on the luscious sensuality of a perfect mouthfeel dish, a slight smile playing upon his lips. "When you get it right, you'll know by how your molars stick together with each bite and how they release. You will sense the different pressures and textures of the food as it is pushed up by your tongue against the roof of your mouth, the way in which it slides down your throat."

I asked him about all those expensive dried ingredients that have no inherent flavor, just interesting textures—like shark fins, sea cucumbers, and swallow nests—things that are usually mentioned whenever the subject of mouthfeel arises. He waved his hand dismissively.

"Unnecessary. The success of mouthfeel depends on the chef's knack for selecting an ingredient of impeccable quality and then cooking it with sufficient moisture, slow heat, and the correct seasoning until it achieves perfection. That is all."

Similar principles behind the concept of mouthfeel were repeated to me again and again by food lovers in Taipei, especially by our older friends, the ones who remembered what it was like to eat back in the decades before their country was stripped to its foundations by invasions and corruption and civil war. Unusually erudite and almost always highly educated, these friends were the literati of Old China, the ones who could still describe in detail how a fine meal should be designed to feed the mind, not just the mouth and the stomach. Slight gentlemen and frail ladies such as these may not have possessed the largest of appetites anymore, but they took extraordinary pleasure in mouthfeel, for it spoke to them and connected them to the ways these foods used to be prepared and appreciated.

Such unusual and sophisticated gastronomic theories had ample time to develop over the centuries simply because China is so huge, so ancient, and has been historically so closed off from the rest of the planet. A unique world of cookery grew up in the land, one that for the longest time was influenced only tangentially by other countries. However, those who over the centuries did manage to cross the Pacific Ocean or Central Asia occasionally found their culinary suggestions welcomed and even assimilated to various degrees into the Middle Kingdom's panoply of cuisines, such as when tandoor ovens came to be used in Guangdong Province to roast dry-rubbed sides of pork and lacquered ducks into southern crispy masterpieces, while cooks in the North learned to wallpaper the insides of these portable kilns with mounds of delicate puff pastry dough, a technique that allows their tops to turn light and airy in the whirling hot air as their bases toast on the rough clay.

China's love for dining well has managed to survive time and upheaval and every misfortune known to mankind, for whenever the swords were sheathed and the soil absorbed the last of the blood and the crops grew once again, her people returned to the dining table and celebrated life as they have since time immemorial. This country possesses one of the oldest of all continuous civilizations on Earth, and that constancy is what has given its inexhaustible—and indefatigable—gastronomes the opportunity to develop concepts like mouthfeel, notions rarely found elsewhere.

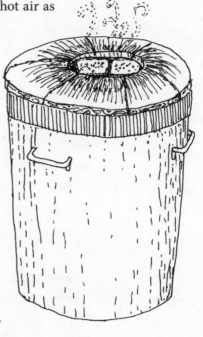

Chinese gourmets have always considered pretty much every living being, flora and fauna alike—with the exception of a fellow human—as being entirely edible and worthy of a chef's attention. This has led to an appreciation for each measure of an animal and each part of a plant, with nothing ever wasted.

One of the greatest talents to which China's masters of *haute cuisine* can lay claim is the ability to eke out fascinating qualities from the lowliest ingredients. For, as that sophisticated old gentleman pointed out, the most elegant mouthfeel dishes do not call for the fanciest or the rarest of items. Those are the concessions cooks often employ to appease their wealthier but irredeemably gauche diners— the ones who measure the quality of their dinner by the size of the bill and the fanciness of their surroundings, the same ones who insist on guzzling overpriced Burgundy with a Cantonese meal or having the chef top their Shanghainese dishes with caviar and foie gras.

True devotees, on the other hand, eagerly seek sensual gratification from the simplest provisions, their only request being that they be prepared correctly, intelligently, and sometimes even subversively. As the author of *The Sui Garden Gastronomy* pointed out, "Bean curd can be made so delicious that it far surpasses swallow nests." And it's true. I've cooked many of his two-hundred-year-old doufu recipes, and they still are winners. I've also eaten swallow nests a couple of times, and while they have an interesting texture, Master Yuan was right on the money about that, too.

A year or two before that Hunanese dinner, when we returned to Taipei from Long Beach at the beginning of the 1980s and I started working at all those cultural institutions, flavors and aromas intrigued me much more than texture, for they were concepts I could easily understand and appreciate. Newbie that I was at the Chinese table, I thought I already knew what made a dish truly great, so I pontificated to the history museum's foreign guests whenever there was a lull in the conversation. To be honest, though, I was still only skating on the surface. And yet by the time of this particular feast, I am already infatuated with the classical Chinese concept of mouth-feel. And that is why I am attempting to ratchet my cooking skills up to a whole new level. I am ready to transcend the passive roles of diner and semicommitted dilettante in order to become even more obsessive and also more than a bit Chinese in the kitchen.

My audience of one loads up my bookshelves with complex tomes that explore food theory and the history of China's magnificent cuisines. I demur as he does this, telling J. H. that my workload already has me too exhausted to struggle through stacks of books written in classical Chinese and reproduced from old editions. But then he'll open one and gleefully show me something that Master Yuan commented on so long ago, his forefinger tracing the forbidding angles of the old-fashioned type as it marches vertically down the page from right to left in tidy columns, and he manages to make those words come alive. Then he'll hand it to me with a little bookmark, and I'll tumble into a whole other way of cooking and eating.

And before I know it, I find myself hungry all over again.

Garlic Chile Sauce (V)

SUÀNRÓNG LÀJIĀOJIÀNG 蒜蓉辣椒醬

J. H. has never loved chiles all that much, but luckily for me, my immediate boss in the library's International Exchange Department showed me how to appreciate China's spiciest foods. Teresa Wang Chang grew up on the mild dishes of Anhui Province and the Yangtze River Delta, but somewhere along the way, she turned into a dedicated chile head. I credit her husband with that, as he is from Guizhou, a heat-loving province located smack between Sichuan and Hunan.

Teresa taught me that chefs often hide homemade chile sauce in the back of their kitchens for their own enjoyment, as well as for favored customers. That is why whenever we sat down for lunch at a place where she was a regular, she'd whisper her request to the server, who would invariably smile conspiratorially before reappearing with the good stuff. However, making chile sauce yourself is not all that hard, and a tiny jar stashed away in a bag—just in case—is my idea of Girl Scout–level preparedness. Be sure to remove the seeds, so the sauce will have a velvety texture. You can also easily halve or quarter this recipe, if you prefer, and then make it fresh as you need it.

8 fat cloves garlic, finely chopped
1 pound | 500 g fresh red chiles of any kind (*see* Tips), seeded and
    finely chopped

1 tablespoon fine sea salt, or more to taste

6 tablespoons | 90 ml vegetable oil, such as peanut or canola

2 teaspoons sugar, or more to taste

Place the garlic and chiles in a medium bowl, sprinkle with the fine sea salt, toss, and let sit for about 5 minutes so that they sweat.

Pour the oil into a wok or a large frying pan and set it over low heat. Add the garlic and chiles and cook slowly for about 10 minutes, stirring every minute or so as they gently bubble away and dissolve into a slightly mushy and aromatic sauce. (Sometimes you just can't get the heat on even your weakest burner down low enough for recipes like this. If that's the case at your house, keep only an edge of the pan on the burner, stir often, and add more oil as needed.) Mix in the sugar, cook for another minute, and then taste. Add more salt or sugar as desired.

Scrape the hot chile sauce into a sterilized 1-cup | 250-ml jar. When the chile sauce has cooled, screw on the cap and refrigerate. *Makes about 1 cup | 250 ml.*

Tips

You can make this as mild or as hot as you like, depending upon the kind of chiles you use. Fresnos are among the mildest, but as you experiment, you can add more fresh red jalapeños or Thai chiles or even fiery-hot habaneros until you reach your sweet spot.

Wear latex gloves when dealing with fresh chiles. Or, chop the chiles and garlic in a food processor.

Chicken Meatballs in Clear Broth

ZHÚJIÉ JĪZHŌNG 竹節雞盅

Traditionally made with squab, this was once one of those pricey Hunanese dishes that only private chefs and the most expensive restaurants could serve in the years that preceded the heady days of Taiwan's high-tech revolution in the late 1970s. But using chicken along with the traditional pork not only makes shopping easier, it also puts this heavenly soup within the reach of most of us. As my friend Marc exclaimed after testing this recipe, "This tastes like a dumpling without the wrapper!"

According to Taiwan's most famous cooking teacher, Fu Pei-mei—whose recipe inspired me to first try my hand at this many long years ago—you should steam the meatballs in bamboo cups. If you do manage to find a dozen, be sure they are absolutely unglazed and free of cracks. But the thing is, I brought some back with me from Taiwan, and as soon as I unpacked them, they split apart with loud pops in our dry California air. So now I just use 8-ounce jelly jars, and no one is ever the wiser, since the soup is decanted into bowls before serving.

Also, the traditional recipe called for whacking the meats together with cleavers, but a food processor makes this task a snap. Just be sure not to add the water chestnuts to the processor—you want to feel and taste those sweet little chunks.

3 ounces | 45 g boneless chicken thigh meat, preferably with skin

3 ounces | 45 g lean pork

4 teaspoons finely minced fresh ginger

2 green onions, white parts only, finely minced

3 cups | 750 ml chicken stock (preferably unsalted, but lightly
  salted is okay), at room temperature

¼ cup | 60 ml Shaoxing rice wine

1½ teaspoons fish sauce

1 teaspoon to 1 tablespoon regular Chinese soy sauce, or to taste

4 fresh or frozen water chestnuts, peeled

Freshly ground black or white pepper

1 teaspoon sugar

Place the chicken and pork in the freezer for about half an hour, until partially frozen; this will make them easier to chop. Set up your steamer, and have six 8-ounce | 250-ml canning jars at hand.

Cut both meats into a fine dice. Transfer to a food processor, add the ginger and green onions, and pulse them together. Because stock (as well as soy sauce) can have wildly varying levels of salt, mix together the stock, rice wine, and fish sauce in a 1-quart | 1-liter measuring cup, and then taste and adjust the seasoning with soy sauce as needed. Pulse about ½ cup | 125 ml of this seasoned stock into the meat mixture so that you can then process it into a really fine paste before scraping this mixture into the measuring cup.

Chop the water chestnuts *by hand* into dice about the size of mung beans—you want them to retain their character, so don't reduce them to mush. Add them to the measuring cup, along with pepper to taste and sugar. Using chopsticks or a whisk, mix the water chestnuts and meat paste into the stock; you will end up with something that looks like a slurry. Do not be dismayed—the magic is yet to come.

Divide the slurry among the jars, stirring it between jars so that you get even amounts of meat, water chestnuts, and stock in each one. Set the jars in the steamer and steam over low heat for 2 hours, refilling the steamer as necessary. (To prepare this ahead of time, steam for only 1 hour, let the jars come to room temperature, and refrigerate them covered; then, steam the jars for another hour just before serving.)

Very gently, so that the delicate meatballs are not disturbed, transfer the contents of each jar into a soup bowl. Serve these piping hot at the end of a great meal. *Serves 6.*

Chapter 8

Entirety

TAIPEI—1984

Our Taiwanese neighbors consider me an oddity. And as the only white person around for miles, I feel it is my duty from time to time to do as little as possible to dispel that notion. Today, for instance, I am dancing in my living room, psyching myself up to go *mano a mano* with a pig's head. As I shuffle away to an old mixtape featuring Koko Taylor and Charles Brown, I glance up at the balcony across the alley. Old Lady Wu is there at her regular perch, leaning over the railing with her chubby wrists crossed, smiling and taking in the action while wrapped in a thick coat, absorbing all of this welcome new grist for the local gossip mill.

I slide across our cold terrazzo floor into the kitchen, primed to get started on something my boyfriend has been begging me to do for ages. I'm red-faced and more than a little sweaty, even though it is an incredibly chilly morning in early spring. Up since before dawn, I have spent the past couple of hours picking up the boned head from the butcher, sharpening knives, setting up my biggest cauldron, prepping and arranging all of the seasonings, and readying the kitchen for a tactical assault on that big fat face. What I am planning to do is nothing short of food voodoo. As I pass the sink, I slip off a rubber glove and, holding my hand against the pig's head, marvel at how close our skin tones are, how similar we are on the surface. I work the glove back on and now feel more than vaguely cannibalistic as I prepare to transform this floppy thing into the semblance of meat.

I know what you are thinking. I even agree with you, for I too questioned my sanity earlier this morning. Staring at the dark ceiling in the hour before sunrise, I silently ran down the list of everything I had to do. And right after that, I pulled my pillow over my head, for the idea of wrestling with a pig's head suddenly didn't sound half as enticing as staying rolled up in a fluffy comforter with my boyfriend softly snoring at my side. As I forced myself out of bed and into an upright position, I told myself that by tomorrow night this would all be worth it, really it would. Besides, I was anxious to see whether I'd in fact succeed. I had been eating the Chinese way for too long now not to know that if the right amount of kitchen witchery is applied, basically any bland ingredient with an interesting texture can be transformed into a wobbly delight that tickles the teeth, challenges perceptions, and reveals a cook's mettle, perhaps even her devotion.

Yes, I tell myself, I'm about to make more than just a meal here—this is going to be something on the order of a graduate thesis on China's traditional culinary aesthetics, but in edible form. I go downstairs and put on my heavy coat and sneakers. As I slip out the front door, I grab two of my mighty string shopping bags, the ones I use for bringing home things like a half-dozen onions, whole chickens, and slabs of ribs. And today, a pig's head.

I'm heading out to meet the butcher's truck on his first pass through our neighborhood. As I turn the corner onto a wider lane, I break into a happy jog, my breath puffing out in little clouds. J. H. and I refer to our butcher fondly (but always out of hearing) as Little Brother Pig, because that is the Chinese children's song he blasts out of the motorcycle-driven cart he putt-putts through our alleys to announce his presence. He is a guy in his midforties with a cigarette perpetually dangling from his lower lip and a voice that is harsh and ragged from calling out his wares for way too many years. As Little Brother Pig swings off his cycle this morning, he limps to the back of his covered flatbed. One of his legs is stiff and bent from a childhood bout with polio, evidence of an epidemic that swept Taiwan years ago. When he sees me, he triumphantly pulls the bone-less pig's head from a cooler near his trays of fresh vegetables, stuffs it in a plastic bag, weighs it, and deposits it ceremoniously into my waiting sack.

"Good morning! I have some fresh sausages, and look at these really beautiful greens." Always the salesman, he waves proudly at his lush display of produce. "So, what else are you in the mood for?" I thank him for saving the day with that beautiful pig's head before passing him some garlic, a clump of fresh ginger, two bunches of green onions, and a hefty bouquet of the flowering garlic stems called scapes.

"Got any caul fat hiding in here?" I ask, anxious as always to have it stashed in the freezer for whenever the desire arises for J. H.'s father's delectable way with steamed fish. Little Brother Pig nods with pride as he digs out a big glob of the webby fat for me. I reach past his trays filled with purple lobes of liver, mahogany kidneys, and coral-shaped brains to take a closer look at the ropes of sweet Taiwan-ese sausages he mentioned, now just begging me to grill them with a handful of whole garlic cloves for sup-per. I can already taste their charred edges in my mind, so four fat links go into my bag, along with a juicy-looking white radish for a simple soup. Dinner tonight will have to

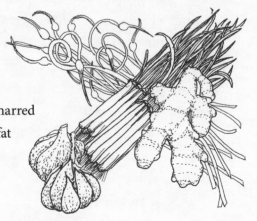

be an especially easy one after such a long day. Thanks to these sausages and radishes, it will be extraordinarily delicious, too.

Up until now, I had always laughingly put off this project by suggesting I make something vastly simpler for dinner, like a banquet of beef Wellington and Yorkshire pudding with a dessert of petits fours, or perhaps a Peking duck feast from tip to tail. But some sort of culinary longing has set in, for J. H. has been wistfully musing more and more frequently about how much he loves *shāchá chǎo zhūtóuròu*, or pig's head stir-fried with Chaozhou's satay sauce.

He rhapsodizes: "Oh, it's so good. You really are missing something."

He sighs: "The soft skin perfectly complements the crisp cartilage, ahhh, and those extraordinarily delicate wisps of meat."

He advises: "The head must be poached in a spiced, heavily salted broth, and then it is chilled, sliced, and stir-fried with the *shāchá*," or satay, that oily reddish seasoning from Chaozhou. Also known as Teochew, this riverport near China's southeastern seacoast is famous for its unique cuisine, which includes stir-fried dishes robed with the unique mixture of ground dried seafood, fried shallots, pulverized chiles, and grated coconut known as satay. "Once the heat of the wok has softened the cold pork just enough to remove the chill and render it supple and silky," he tells me, "the sauce and other condiments should be tossed in so that they can robe each piece with a gentle punch of flavor."

He murmurs: "If we could manage to hunt down some fresh scapes, their subtle garlic flavor will perfectly temper the sauce and

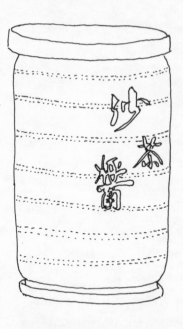

highlight the natural sweetness of the pork. That green would be a welcome bit of color in there, too."

He wheedles: "How nice it would be to finally enjoy this dish again after so, so many years. And," he adds by way of a coda, as if the thought had just occurred to him, unbidden, "with the earliest scapes just coming into the market, now is the perfect time."

J. H. has all the subtlety of a hammer upside the head, but I have to admit that this does sound unbelievably good. I checked my calendar last week and started planning. Tomorrow is a holiday and today is free. Since some food-loving friends are supposed to come over the next evening for dinner, I've given in to his not-so-subtle nagging as much out of curiosity as a resigned sop to conjugal accord.

He didn't happen to rave over the scrubbing part, or even mention it in passing. And for good reason. Cleaning a pig's entire face takes forever, which I suppose is the reason why no restaurant bothers to offer this anymore. I feel a seditious rage surging every few minutes as I tussle with the thing. It's cold and clammy, and fat coats my gloves whenever I touch the edges, making the head slipperier and my array of tools even more dangerous. I've propped it up against one corner of a plastic tub set in the sink so I can steady it for a scrupulous cleaning, something that right about now looks more like a high-end spa service than butchery. Heavy-duty steel tweezers, needle-nose pliers, a paring knife, paper towels, an old toothbrush, a bowl of coarse salt, a Lady Bic razor, and a pile of Q-tips form my pile of tools. We only have cold water in our kitchen, so I'm chilled all the way down to my toes after half an hour of working.

Little Brother Pig's supplier did a good once-over-lightly when he prepped it, but I will still have to completely scour the (more or less) hairless exterior by vigorously brushing salt into every little fold in order to remove the residual piggy grime. Once it has been rinsed, I grab the unwieldy head with a paper towel to keep it from slipping out of my hands and start on the left side of the face, inserting Q-tips in the crevices and holes to nudge away at things I don't want to think about too much.

I stare at the pig, and it stares back at me. Now it's time to excavate the right ear canal. I grimly reach for another cotton swab and go to work, cussing under my breath.

THIS KITCHEN, despite its drawbacks, is the best we have ever had. The last one, in our third-floor walkup in the Shipai District, was a tiny ship-like galley consisting of little more than a small counter against the outside wall to hold a propane stovetop, work area, plates, everything. Two people could not pass each other in there without provoking a fistfight. Now at last I have a room that is big enough for me to cook in while my fastidious boyfriend cleans up around me, under me, and after me. Around six feet by ten, the kitchen is so enormous by Chinese standards that both a table and a refrigerator share a space along the wall opposite the counter and sink, both of which are completely covered in dinged white tiles.

The single window over the sink usually gives me a calming view of the plants out back as I work, but today the glass remains firmly shut against the cold, and it is completely fogged up from my breath. Most days when it's warmer, I wrestle it open for a breeze to augment the tiny wall fan stuck up high over the stove. Many years' worth of grease around the vent were dabbed with paint before we moved in, and the fan vibrates noisily from the extra weight, but nevertheless I remain elated by the kitchen's size and seemingly limitless potential.

As a longtime sucker for farmhouse pottery and wooden utensils, I've tacked Technicolor-hued oilcloth on the shelves to hold a collection that is as decorative as it is useful. Whenever I can, I rummage through the local hardware stores in search of old things no one wants anymore, kitchen stuff that is passé to most eyes: plates with blue peonies around the edge, rice bowls that have indigo netting on the inside, and thick pottery noodle bowls decorated with blue bamboo leaves on the outside. My most prized kitchen possession is a serving bowl I found in an antiques store in a nearby port, the lovely little village of Tamsui. A cobalt phoenix in audacious swirls decorates its vintage gray exterior and bubbled

glaze. Costing all of ten bucks, it looks like a student of Picasso could very well have made it during a vacation in Taipei. Next to it are six sky-blue juice glasses; their ribbed surfaces catch the light and add sparkle to the shelves alongside our pressed-glass bowls. Bamboo chopsticks are propped up in a blue-lined vase. I seem to like blue.

A small table just big enough for two is where we eat in this kitchen, and a dining table bookended with benches outside the kitchen door offers seating for eight, or ten if we really squeeze. Spatulas and spoons stick out of a clay jar on the tile counter next to the two-burner wok stove. The propane tank beneath it props up a big bag of rice, and next to it in the cool, dark cubby are large jars where I ferment things, such as bean curd cheese and rice wine and pickles, as well as smaller containers for brined eggs and seasoned oils.

The previous week, I made a big batch of my favorite chile oil and its lusciously goopy solids as I formulated my own plans for this damned pig's head. The boyfriend will have his satay-robed dish, of course, but the day after tomorrow—when the guests have left and life has returned to normal—the chilled braised ears will be finely shredded and then tossed with a small mountain of julienned green onions, cilantro, and cucumbers, a touch of soy sauce and black vinegar, and a healthy spoonful of the crunchy layer at the bottom of

my chile oil. Sprinkled with toasted sesame seeds and served with a cold beer, this will be a just reward for my toils. As I think of this, my hunger makes me willing to dive down into the bottom of this particular ear and scrub it even more mercilessly.

Gruesome as this work is, my mood lightens considerably once the sun comes up over the roofs to my left, causing light to pour into the kitchen window and refract around the room. I crack open the window and watch the birds chatter and hop along the concrete wall only a few steps from where I stand. We have called this place home for more than a thousand days already. It's a part of us. It looks lived-in and well loved. Our books are stacked everywhere, and all the other rooms smell of paper and sunlight. The kitchen, on the other hand, almost always has the aroma of something tasty bouncing around inside.

This is the first time since I moved out of my mother's home at the end of high school that I've been part of a neighborhood, the first time I've had my own yard, the first time I've ever considered the place I sleep as my home. Here the combination of extended families and front yards where people hang out with the gates open on hot nights means that everybody pretty much knows everyone else's business. And my business is apparently the most interesting one of all, at least to Old Lady Wu.

THE MAJORITY OF our neighbors are Wus, for the simple reason that a couple of decades ago, these rows of cheaply made townhouses arose out of the lands of an extensive farm belonging to a Taiwanese clan.

As a consequence, we rent our place from one of the descendants. Our landlord is a sleek, chubby guy who lives in the alley behind us. Mr. Wu revels in his sudden affluence by wearing gold chains and squeezing his big Caddy down our wall-lined lanes. However, the older folks continue to act as though they are still barely eking by, sort of like my grandparents' Great Depression generation. Our landlord's father is a hog farmer who gets about before dawn on a rusty bicycle, dresses in rags, and tips our communal slop buckets into the big plastic barrels he has strapped behind his seat. Mr. Wu Senior sneers at his son's extravagance, or at least that's what he seems to be saying whenever he grumbles at me in Taiwanese.

One of the preeminent elders here in the Land of Wu lives catty-corner from us; I refer to her here as Old Lady Wu, but everyone else calls her Grandma. She's the matriarch of our alley. Apparently I'm the only foreigner she has ever met, and as she is the self-appointed guardian of public safety and the ultimate supervisor of private doings on our block, she parks herself in a housedress on her balcony whenever the weather is good, leans forward, and stares into my living room, anxiously waiting for me to do something strange.

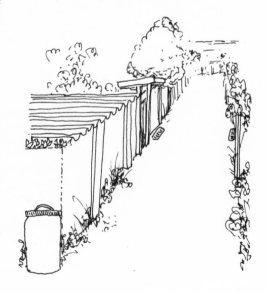

The first time I met her was in my living room. I had just finished sweeping under the sofa when I turned around to find her standing in front of me. I brandished my broom at her as I screamed. I then yelled in Mandarin, "How did you get in?"

Old Lady Wu chuckled at me and said in Taiwanese, "I don't speak Mandarin." Still shaking, I repeated my question in a combination of Mandarin and sign language. She laughed again and pointed at my formerly locked gate, which was standing wide open, as if to say, *How else?* Old Lady Wu wandered around the downstairs, picking up things along the way for closer inspection and chatting away at me in Taiwanese. I put down my broom and tried smiling brightly while attempting to corral her toward the front door. She was having none of it. Books were rifled and pillows poked. My neighbor opened the refrigerator, inspected a couple of leftovers, and sized up my jars of preserved ingredients.

"What's this?" she asked, waving a jar of instant coffee at me. I told her and she checked that out, too. Chuckling some more, she

said something and punched me in the arm on her way out of the kitchen. I had no idea what that meant. "I am now going to look upstairs," she announced, or at least I think that's what she said. I ran over to the staircase and blocked her way, saying in a tortured mish-mash of Mandarin and Taiwanese, "Messy up there it is, Grandma. Please. No can allow you to perceive it. Embarrassing. No. Um, very. Please." She tried to elbow her way past me, but I eventually half-shoved, half-slid her across the floor.

"You must come back some other time," I tried to tell her as I finally manhandled her out the door, "when I've had time to tidy up for an honored guest such as yourself." Once that was accomplished with lots of smiles and bowing, and I had confirmed that she was safely back in her own yard, I took a closer look at my gate and real-ized she had stuck her hand underneath it and somehow jimmied it open. Old Lady Wu was evidently not to be trifled with. I hammered a big nail into the bolt on the fixed side of the gate so that I'd have no more unannounced visitations.

She now contents herself by keeping an eye on me from a distance, and I reciprocate by occasionally giving her something to look at.

WHEN I FIRST arrived in Taipei, squeamishness would have pre-vented me from even looking at a pig's head, much less considering it food. I would have testified to anyone within hearing range that shelling out good money in order to grapple with it in a basin full of cold water at the crack of dawn was a masochistic enterprise of the first order. But things have changed quite a bit in my life over the past six years, and by *things* I mean me.

Around midmorning, my pig's head is finally squeaky clean. It glistens under the kitchen's fluorescent tubes as I cut off its ears down at the base, since these thin flaps will cook in a shorter amount of time than the thick face. The whole head and ears get blanched for about ten minutes to release any impurities, and then I pour out the scummy water and rinse them thoroughly. This step also opens up the pores so that I can provide the final depilatory amenities to what was once a brutally hirsute animal. Thick bristles get yanked out with the pliers and the thinner hairs are tweezed, and the skin is then shaved until it is as smooth as a baby's bum. My hard work and the mad rush to get things done are now officially over.

Savoring a mug of hot oolong tea as I admire my handiwork, I decide to relax in the front yard under the poinsettia while a fresh cauldron of water slowly comes to a boil. When I hear cries in Taiwanese for *dau hui,* I flag down another regular hawker of breakfast foods: the Taiwanese lady who pushes a cart filled with a massive steaming wooden bucket of the pudding known in Mandarin as *dòuhuā,* which is gently coagulated soy milk. While she readies her flattish ladle and opens up the wooden lid, I run inside to fetch some money, as well as a pan so that she can slide the delicate wedges directly in there before ladling gingery syrup and boiled peanuts on top. The day is already starting to look up.

Back in the kitchen, I toss a large handful of salt and some whole star anise into the boiling water. Aromatics are very important at this point, for they will tame the gaminess of the pork and freshen the aromas. Into the pot go stick cinnamon, fennel seeds, cloves of garlic, Sichuan and black peppercorns, a smacked cluster of fresh ginger, and a bunch of whole green onions, along with a good glug of the local white lightning called sorghum liquor, or *gāoliáng*. These will shimmy their way into every cell, and since almost all of the seasonings are considered "warming" in Chinese medicine, they will also counteract the inherent coolness of the pork skin. Balance is achieved, and this will be passed on to those who partake of these dishes. The recipe is thus structured in terms of not only how the dish will taste, smell, and feel, but also how it will affect the diners' bodies and moods. How is this not culinary sorcery?

Two hours later, I fish out the ears and set them aside. Their cartilage is tender enough to be pierced with a fingernail. Another sixty minutes goes by, and a chopstick inserted into the thickest part of the cheek slides through as if it were made of butter. Using a wok spatula and a heavy slotted spoon, I transfer the head with its now-translucent skin to a waiting bowl. I pick off and discard the spices and aromatics, their scents long gone and their work done. I run my fingers gently over the ears and face so that I can pluck out any errant hairs. The pork steams on the counter, but after only an hour in the chilly kitchen air it is cool enough to transfer to the refrigerator. I take this opportunity to pass out on the sofa.

The next evening, about two hours before our guests are set to arrive, I wash that bunch of green flowering garlic stalks, trim off their buds filled with spiky blossoms, and chop the tender stems on the diagonal into inch-long lengths. Their perfume summons J. H. downstairs and into the kitchen. As always, he whistles when he knows that he's about to get fed. I kid him about it, but this never seems to stop him. The anticipation he feels for tonight's dish has him bouncing on his toes, fussing around the kitchen, and whistling something from *Turandot*.

"I'll cut up the head, all right?" he asks me. He already has the chopping block out and our sharpest knife at the ready, so this is more a polite gesture than a question. He lovingly slices off an edge of the cheek, cuts it in half, and offers me a piece. Its chill hits my tongue, and then the shard softens in the warmth of my mouth. Beneath the pillowy skin, the fat has escaped, leaving behind only a buttery sensation that is known as *yóuérbùni* (meaning "creamy but not greasy"). All those spices and aromatics weave through the layers and are released by the pressure of my teeth. The flavor is just salty enough to punch through the porkiness, while the sorghum liquor has erased the scent of the barnyard. The skin is silky and the meat puddles against my tongue. J. H. caresses the small of my back in thanks and lifts up my chin for a kiss, his fingers leaving behind little skids of scented oil.

I set the table and start to cook a pot of rice while the sun goes down behind the house next door. We are just finishing up the preparations when our guests ring the doorbell. I usher them in and set out snacks and drinks in the dining room before returning to the kitchen. My guy has happily reduced half of the head into a small mountain of beige shavings. I get out the wok, set it over high heat, drizzle in a little oil and a pinch of salt, and then quickly stir-fry the garlic scapes. After that I scrape them into a work bowl so that J. H. can prepare the rest of the dish. From the doorway, I watch him assuaging his cravings at last as he barely heats through the pork in the wok before tossing it with the brick-hued satay sauce and other seasonings. In the final seconds, he adds the scapes to create a jumble of green and red strips. When he is pleased with how they taste, he scoops it all into the phoenix bowl and carries it proudly to the dining room table. All that hard work disappears into our mouths as we laugh, toast each other with beer and more *gāoliáng*, and tell stories.

I remember my mother saying something about not being able to make a silk purse out of a sow's ear. I do believe she got that wrong.

The Bean Curd of Jiang Dailang

JiĂng DàiLáng dòufǔ 蔣侍郎豆腐

As the author of *The Sui Garden Gastronomy*, Yuan Mei had a lot to say about food, but he also never pulled any punches when he blasted boorish diners and slovenly cooks. He has been compared to various French food writers, but for my money he calls to mind Fernand Point, as both Master Yuan's book and *Ma Gastronomie* are pithy, opinionated, short, and fun to read. However, while Chef Point was a professional restaurateur and is considered the father of modern French cuisine, Master Yuan was a member of the literati, so he spent considerably more time at the dining table than in the kitchen.

Master Yuan went out of his way to extol the virtues of cooking with simple, honest ingredients. He has a good handful of recipes in *The Sui Garden Gastronomy* for bean curd, and this one has become a family favorite. Here is the original version:

Remove the skin from both sides of the bean curd, and then cut each square into sixteen slices. Dry these slightly. Heat rendered lard until it starts to smoke and add the bean curd. Sprinkle with a pinch of fleur de sel and turn the slices over, and add one teacup of sweet wine plus one hundred twenty large dried shrimp; if you do not have large dried shrimp, use three hundred small dried shrimp. First cover the dried shrimp with boiling water and soak for two hours, add one small cup aged soy sauce and let it come again to a boil for a while, then add a pinch of sugar and let it come to a boil for a while, add one hundred twenty pieces of thin green onions cut into half-inch lengths, and gently plate.

Now here is our version, which is a supremely homey dish—and surprisingly savory, rather than fishy, which this much dried shrimp might lead you to otherwise expect. Like the Bear Paw Doufu on page 66, the directions here ask you to drain the bean curd slices before frying them, an inspired step that turns a supremely vegetarian ingredient into something almost meaty.

12 medium (¾-inch | 2 cm) or 24 small (½-inch | 1.25 cm) dried shrimp

1 block (about 14 ounces | 300 g) firm bean curd

¼ cup | 60 ml rendered lard (best) or unsalted butter

½ teaspoon sea salt

½ cup | 125 ml water

¼ cup | 60 ml Shaoxing rice wine

2 tablespoons regular Chinese soy sauce

About 1 teaspoon rock sugar

4 green onions, trimmed, halved lengthwise, and cut into 1 inch | 2 cm lengths

Place the dried shrimp in a heatproof bowl, cover with boiling water, and set a plate on top of the bowl to cover it. Let stand for at least 2 hours, and up to overnight, then drain the shrimp and pick off any shells or dark areas, including the sandy veins; rinse them well.

Cut the bean curd lengthwise in half and then crosswise into slices about ½ inch | 1.25 cm thick. Lay these on a kitchen towel to wick up excess moisture, then flip them over to dry the other side.

Set an 8-inch | 20-cm frying pan over medium heat, add the lard or butter, and let it melt. When the oil is hot, arrange the bean curd in the skillet in a single layer and sprinkle with the flaky sea salt. When the bean curd is browned on the bottom and moves easily when you poke it, flip it over and brown the other side.

Pour off most of the fat from the pan. Scatter the shrimp over the bean curd. Add the water, rice wine, soy sauce, sugar, and water to the pan and bring the liquid to a full boil, then lower the heat to maintain a simmer and loosely cover the frying pan. As soon as most of the sauce has evaporated—20 to 30 minutes—add the green onions, cover again, and cook just until they are wilted. Turn over the bean curd—the bottoms should be a luscious brown by now—and scoot everything onto a platter. Rice and perhaps a vegetable would be the perfect accompaniments. *Serves 4.*

Smoked Trotters

XŪN ZHŪJIĂO 薰豬腳

Finding a quality butcher who will sell you a whole pig's head, or even my favorite parts—the ears and the jowls—can be particularly challenging. You would think that pig's feet would be easier to order, but sometimes these too can be hard to hunt down. However, that is a quest worth pursuing, for this way with trotters might just end up being among the most sensuous things you'll ever eat.

The skin is like smoky, luxurious silk wrapped around a complex collection of bones and tendons, with just a touch of meat to hold things together. When these feet are cooked correctly—and by that I mean that they are blanched properly, braised until perfectly tender, seasoned with restraint, and then smoked into culinary nirvana—few things are better to munch on while contemplating how wonderful life can be.

A stovetop smoker is perfect for creating this type of dish. These are relatively inexpensive and will prove to be a great investment if you adore smoked foods as much as we do. As always, make sure the pig comes from a responsible farmer who gave the animal a great life. What you want for that pig is what we should wish for anybody: a happy existence ending with one really fast, really bad day.

6 pig's trotters, preferably free-range and of the highest quality
(*see* Tips), cut up by your butcher as directed below

BRAISE

½ cup | 50 g thinly sliced fresh ginger

6 green onions, trimmed but otherwise left whole

¼ cup | 60 ml regular Chinese soy sauce

½ cup | 125 ml Shaoxing rice wine

1 piece of rock sugar, about the size of an egg

2 star anise

Half a stick of cinnamon

SMOKE

Spray oil

¼ cup | 50 g raw rice, or more as needed

¼ cup | 60 g sugar, or more as needed

¼ cup | 8 g dry tea leaves, or more as needed

¼ cup lightly packed | 10 g dry jamaica (hibiscus) flowers, or
more as needed, optional

Have your butcher use a band saw to slice each trotter in half length-wise and then make 2 or 3 crosscuts, giving you 4 to 6 pieces per foot. Clean the feet carefully, pat them dry with a paper towel, and poke around in the crevasses of the skin in search of hairs or anything else that requires your attention.

Place the feet in a large pot or Dutch oven, cover with water, and bring this to a full boil before lowering the heat to maintain a good simmer. Cook the feet for around 10 minutes to remove any impurities, then drain and rinse off the feet and pan. Return the feet to the pan, cover them with fresh water, bring the water to a full boil again, and then simmer the feet until the skin feels soft and you can pierce through the thickest piece with a chopstick—about 45 minutes—topping off the pan with more boiling water as needed.

Add all of the braising ingredients to the pot or Dutch oven. Simmer the feet in this liquid for around 3 hours, until it has been reduced to around ½ inch | 1 cm or so at the bottom. Remove the pan from the heat and cool the feet on a platter. Use the strained leftover sauce for something else, such as a seasoning for blanched vegetables or stir-fries. You can make the feet ahead of time up to this point and then refrigerate.

To smoke the pork, spray the tray of your stovetop smoker with oil. Line the fuel bowl with a piece of foil before filling it with half of the rice, sugar, tea leaves, and optional jamaica flowers. Set the rack on top of the smoker and arrange around half of the pork pieces on it. You don't want to pack things in there, otherwise the smoke will not be able to circulate freely. Turn the overhead fan on your stove up to high and set the smoker over high heat.

When smoke comes billowing out, cover the smoker, lower the heat to medium-low, and smoke the feet for 10 minutes. Turn off the heat, but leave the smoker covered and on the burner. After about 15 minutes, check the pork: it should be a glorious mahogany brown and smell magnificent. Repeat with the rest of the fuel and pork until all of the feet have been smoked. Serve them hot or slightly warm. These can be reheated if wrapped in foil and warmed in a 325°F | 160°C oven for about 15 minutes. *Serves 8 to 12 as a bar snack or appetizer, 4 to 6 as an entrée with soup noodles or steamed rice.*

Chapter 9

Perplexity

LOS ANGELES—1992 AND 1996
(AND MAINLAND CHINA—1936 TO 1949)

J. H.'s father looks over his glasses at the oblique chunks of bean curd piling up in front of me. He frowns slightly and gently clears his throat, for, unlike his small squadron of perfectly hollowed-out pyramids, my disheveled army is most definitely not up to his exacting standards. It isn't that he expects much from me, the inappropriately foreign girlfriend of his eldest son, but I am definitely irritating him more than usual today as we prepare his annual Chinese New Year's Eve extravaganza.

"You are going too fast," he says at last in his Cantonese-accented Mandarin. "Watch me."

I try to rationalize why it should always take forever to cook a meal in his tiny apartment kitchen. Firecrackers rip and rebound though the alleys, and wisps of gunpowder filter in through a begrudgingly opened crack in his living room window. The bustle of Chinatown's traffic vibrates thirteen stories below us, the flat pale blue of the Los Angeles sky casting harsh afternoon shadows on his brushes and pots of ink. I take in a deep breath to calm myself, but I have to stifle a sneeze from the heavy odor of sandalwood soap that always permeates his rooms.

This is the last day of the Year of the Ram. We are visiting J. H.'s father from our place in Northern California, where we moved in 1985 after packing up our lives in Taipei. I'm here to help him prepare the family's New Year's Eve feast that will welcome the Year of the Monkey, which starts tomorrow, and have happily volunteered once again for kitchen duty. As long as I am safely tucked away in his basic kitchenette, I will get to eat well while absorbing whatever secrets the family's top chef decides to impart that year.

As always, I am on my best behavior with J. H.'s father—not as wary as with his volcanic wife, just very mindful of our generational and cultural differences. He patiently shows me again what it is that I should be doing: A fingertip slips into the yielding mass and then scoops up microscopic bits as he carefully prods away, hollowing out the doufu triangle with infinite care so that its sides are not breached. He readies them so that they can be stuffed with marbles of ground pork seasoned in the style of his Hakka hometown in Guangdong hill country. He was forced to abandon this ancient ancestral fold when civil war exiled him from the Mainland, along with his wife and children, first to Taiwan and then to the States. As he enters his ninth decade, these deeply savory Hakka dishes tether him to the past and in turn form the sole connections any of us will ever have to his former life.

JUST AS WE REFER to certain communities, traditions, and foods as being Jewish, the name *Hakka* is used to label a people, heritage, and cuisine, rather than a particular locale, for the Hakka most likely are the descendants of waves of northern refugees who, around a thousand years ago, landed south of the Chang Jiang, far out of reach of most wars and famines and unrest. But since all the good lands had long since been snapped up down there, the newcomers were often forced to settle in the South's stony hills, in places that gave them little more than an opportunity to endure thankless lifetimes of toil as miners and subsistence farmers. These lands offered so little by way of desirability that the locals figured the newcomers would give up before long and move away, which is why they referred to them in Cantonese as *haak gaa*, or guest families.

However, the newcomers stayed. Toughing it out is pretty much the defining characteristic of Hakka culture, and their food is a reflection of this practicality. Meat, fish, and poultry are usually ground up, extended with fillers, used as seasonings, and mentioned in passing rather than considered the center of a meal. Nevertheless, the flavors here are deep and full, thanks to preserved vegetables such as Chinese radishes and various types of mustard leaves that are wilted in the sun, salted, and then given time to slowly ferment and develop into semidried pickles. With the exception of a few feast days, vegetables and grains define the menu and fill up the stomach, making Hakka cuisine a healthful and delicious way to eat.

These creations can at times be stunning. My favorite is composed of long beans twisted around plump balls of finely minced fish. They look otherworldly, and yet, like most things Hakka, long-bean wreaths are a study in practicality combined with inventiveness. The relatively tiny bit of protein here is transformed into something that can feed a big family, the fish dwarfed by all those vegetables in a very beautiful way. In fact, the first time you encounter them, these wreaths may appear more like macramé knickknacks than food. But then again, that is part of their charm.

Long beans are nothing more than the slender pods in which a variety of cowpea grows, and because these vegetables can reach a yard in length, they are sometimes referred to as *snake beans* or *yardlong beans*. The pods are tender as long as they are picked at just the right time, which is while the seeds are still soft and embryonic. Long beans are similar in taste and texture to string beans, and even though these wreaths look impossibly difficult to make, all that is required is that a blanched bean be looped around itself to form a circle. Ground fish is combined with eggs and starch to lighten it and also to extend the protein just that much farther. This filling is stuffed into the center of the wreaths, which are then pan-fried and garnished with a sauce. It's simple, direct food, and yet at the same time incredibly inspired.

In Hakka cooking, absolutely nothing ever goes to waste. J. H. remembers watching his father beat pig's lungs with a wooden mallet, one of the first steps in their preparation. All those little air sacs—sort of like layers and layers of bubble wrap—had to be popped before he could use his mother's recipe to create something intensely savory for the dinner table. I never fail to marvel at how the Hakka manage to turn even what looks to be superficially inedible into the kind of comfort food that satisfies the deepest of aches.

Such attention to thriftiness, though, can have its downside. When J. H. was still young, he was invited to the house of one of his father's distant older cousins, a wealthy and imposing man and the senior male in his father's generation, which made him pretty much the head of that particular crop of Huangs. He had deep-set eyes, the brown irises ringed with blue, as well as three wives who looked almost exactly alike—small and plump in contrast to his tall and lanky physique—and close to twenty children. But J. H. didn't really care about all that. He was there for one thing and one thing only: their household's legendary smoked chicken. And smoked chicken was going to be on the menu.

J. H. could barely contain his excitement at finally getting to dine on the touted culinary masterpiece of his father's clan. The minutes dragged by as he tried to dredge up conversation with this daunting man, one of the few people his father ever spoke of with awe. Finally, lunch was announced. J. H. scrambled to the dining table, as excited as everyone else for this rare treat. A singularly petite bird was finally served with a flourish, already whacked up into slivers so everyone could have a taste.

"It was gone in a flash," he mourns to this day. "I don't remember even tasting it."

Along with a handful of other officials, this uncle ran one of Taiwan's five government branches, the Examination Yuan, which is responsible for overseeing management of the island's civil servants. But then again, accomplishments as commendable as his were considered not all that unusual among Hakka men, for some went on to even greater achievements, such as the Chinese Republic's founding father Sun Yat-sen, Singapore's longtime prime minister Lee Kwan Yew, and one of Mainland China's chief military commanders, General Zhu De. Higher education was, as always, the most proven path to success, and promising Hakka boys were taught to aim for the stars.

Hakka girls were, with few exceptions, forever tied to the land and so never had their feet broken and bound. They—along with those men who became laborers for one reason or another—were fated to toil their entire lives with bent backs and calloused hands. The first time I witnessed this was when I came across a construction gang working on the roads in northern Hong Kong in 1977. I was traveling through the New Territories, which at the time constituted an undeveloped buffer with the Mainland. China was still embroiled in the last throes of the Cultural Revolution, so this was as close as I could get to the very much closed-off border. Weathered women in broad woven hats bordered with a couple of inches of dark fabric fringe carved out the hillside with pickaxes and shovels. Dressed all in black, many had gray hair dangling down into their heavily crinkled and tanned faces. I asked the person seated next to me on the bus who they were and discovered that these women were Hakka. As we passed by, some of them looked up at me and smiled. I smiled back, but never in a million years would I have bet that before long I'd be at least tangentially related to them, that I'd be part of a Hakka family, too.

THE HUANGS who brought J. H.'s father into the world lived for ages in a county called Longchuan, or Dragon River, up on the northern border of Guangdong Province. This craggy land has been continually inhabited since prehistoric times, but sometime during the last millennia or two the Hakka people took over this territory and called it home. Most of their forebears traveled south from the Central Plains near the Yellow River, and J. H.'s father told him that the clan's ancestors had once lived in the ancient imperial capital of Luoyang in Henan Province. But I discovered in a roundabout way that his branch of the Huangs can also be traced all the way to the deeply rippled landscape of western Fujian Province, where the clan's most famous ancestor lived more than a thousand years ago. Chinese families have traditionally recorded the male line back to its earliest known beginnings in massive *jiāpǔ*, or genealogies, and yet in the Huang family, a strange keepsake—a poem—was added to its complex family history, and it is something that to this day links all the progeny together.

This early ancestor of record, Huang Qiaoshan, grew up in Hepingzhen, a village so tiny that even today only a few still call it home

in this country of more than a billion people. His great-grandfather had migrated south to there from Gushi in Henan, very probably during the emperor's military campaigns against local warlords in the early 800s. More than a hundred years later, Huang Qiaoshan was awarded grand titles from his emperor, such as Marquis of a Thousand Households, in appreciation for his efforts in quashing bandits and suppressing civil disorder during the waning years of the Tang dynasty. He was a poet and a scholar who had founded the renowned Heping Academy, a school that numbered many illustrious men among its graduates, but—even more important to this story at least—is the fact that Huang Qiaoshan was a highly prolific patriarch. His three wives probably blessed him with daughters, but of course no mention has ever been made of them. Instead, what we do know is that he eventually found himself surrounded by twenty-one grown sons and an impressive contingent of even younger male offspring.*

Emperors rose and fell quickly during this particularly tumultuous era, as can be seen from its official name: the Five Dynasties and Ten Kingdoms. When the last of the Later Han dynasty emperors was murdered in 951 and the country dissolved into utter chaos, Huang Qiaoshan decided that the best way to preserve the male line would be to transplant his descendants far and wide. So, on an auspicious day that same year, he sent eighteen of them and all their children out into the world—everyone except for the eldest son by each wife and their

---

* With this many descendants, it's no wonder that the odds of finding Chinese people with Huang Qiaoshan in their ancestry are actually as easy as reaching out on a Chinese street and grabbing whoever walks by. Assuming that only two offspring were produced over forty generations, this would give Huang Qiaoshan more than one trillion descendants—and that's erring on the extreme side of restraint. What it comes down to, I guess, is that Chinese people are as interrelated as white people are, for it is said that almost everyone with European blood can pretty much claim Charlemagne as their great-times-forty grandfather. Having the whole world as interrelated as this, one would think we would all get along like family. But then again, maybe that's the problem.

immediate families—and gave them copies of his "Poem on Recognizing the Ancestors," which predicts they will set down roots in strange lands and encourages them to remember their forebears.

Those eighteen sons sought quiet lands as far away as possible from the country's civil wars, and it is entirely probable that many ended up alongside other newcomers in China's South to create the world's largest pocket of Hakkas, one that lies inside a vast inland triangle of corrugated land where southwestern Fujian, southeastern Jiangxi, and northeastern Guangdong meet. The mountain roads up there are riddled with switchbacks, and the names of many settlements speak of tough lives, of hardscrabble miners and farmers: Snake Pit, Stone Pit, Puppy Pit, Sandy Bottom, Gravel Fields, Dragon Bone Acre. Cut off from the rest of the world by steep mountains and rushing rivers, these villages became tiny pockets of civilization consumed with old traditions and even older ways of doing things. As in Appalachia, this led to a wariness of strangers, an almost classical way of speaking, and the sort of insular dialects that only isolation can create. The Hakka are frugal because they have to be. They are clannish because clan members are the only people they know. They keep to themselves because they never had any other choice.

An elaborate Hakka version of the Hatfields and McCoys feud pretty much ties a bow on this picture. It all started only a couple

認祖詩
駿馬登程往異方，任從隨地立綱常。
身居外境猶吾境，家住他鄉則故鄉。
朝夕莫忘親命語，晨昏須薦祖宗香。
漫云富貴由天定，三七男兒當自強。

of generations ago in the village where J. H.'s father grew up, when a Zhang child let the family water buffalo graze among the Huang clan's tombs. The Huangs took umbrage at having cow dung plopped on their ancestors' heads, and some took it upon themselves to, shall we say, physically school the child. The Zhangs couldn't stand for that, naturally, and soon there were no more conversations, no more intermarriage, and no more interactions other than flying fists and bullets.

The curious element is that this deep-seated animosity came full circle with J. H.'s family many decades later during the tail end of the 1940s, when they were living in Guangdong's capital, Guangzhou. His parents befriended a Doctor Zhang and his wife—nice people, salt of the earth, Hakka from the same general vicinity as the Huangs, and by the way childless. The Zhangs took an instant liking to J. H.'s pretty youngest sister, Little Three, and, as they longed to have a daughter, proposed one day that they take the toddler off her parents' hands. Harried by her small herd of kids, J. H.'s mother probably said something on the order of "Help yourselves." The thrilled Zhangs wasted no time in readying a room for Little Three. As soon as J. H.'s father got wind of this, he went over and explained that his wife hadn't meant it, that they really loved their baby girl and didn't want to let her go. And that broke the hearts of the Zhangs, who then hated the Huangs. And thus the Zhang–Huang cycle of animosity got underway all over again. Some things are just meant to be, I guess.

THE DIRECT ANCESTORS of my boyfriend's clan made their home about sixty miles west as the crow flies from the capital of Hakka life, the city of Meizhou. J. H.'s paternal grandfather, Huang Rushan, had graduated from law school before becoming the county governor in a village called Laolong on the East River. As the eldest son, J. H.'s father, Huang Longjin (his given name means "Dragon's Gold"), was destined to assume this country throne and live a life defined by traditional ways. With this in mind, his father selected a young country girl to be his teenage heir's first wife, a suitable someone-or-other who would then work in the fields, bear him sons, and put up with whatever he and life threw her way.

However, Laolong was so isolated that no one had factored a world war into this calculation. And so, while the two families celebrated the upcoming nuptials, Japanese bombs fell and invading troops laid waste to China's Northeast. During the years that Hitler gradually rose to power in Europe, the Japanese Empire was busy instituting its own crazed version of the Monroe Doctrine—what they called the Greater East Asia Co-Prosperity Sphere—over much of East and Southeast Asia. The real prize in Japan's expansionist dreams had always been China's vast resources and endless supply of labor; by the 1930s, conquest of the Middle Kingdom at last seemed tantalizingly within reach. Endless civil war, warlord rule, and famine had rocked China throughout this decade, and Japan took full advantage of this by first seizing Manchuria in the Northeast, and then many of the northern provinces. China was under siege, and its young men and women took up arms. Huang Longjin ran away to join the Nationalist Air Force, but time and history never gave him the chance to return as a war hero, as a stunningly successful prodigal son, as a brave aviator with a beautiful bride on his arm and a cluster of children to show off. In fact, he never even got to apologize or try to mend fences, for one day his father, Huang Rushan, and his mother, Zhong Yunjie, were hauled into the village square, charged with being antirevolutionary bourgeoisie, and shot on the spot.

Huang Longjin passed the entry exams for the Guangdong Air Force Academy somewhere around 1934.* Basic training led to flight school, and by 1937 he was a crack fighter pilot. Fast, lucky, and so good at striking down his prey that fellow aviators gave him the English nickname "Tiger," he took part in endless sorties as he piloted a simple biplane against the enemy's nimbler aircraft, including shooting down a Japanese fighter plane near Changshou in Sichuan. Luck has a well-earned reputation for ducking out at the most inconvenient times, though. One such lapse occurred when the belly of his plane was hit by machine-gun fire as he assaulted a Japanese bomber. He was angling away from the sortie when shrapnel tore into the bottom of his boot, and to the end of his days he bore a deep scar down the middle of his left foot.

But Huang Longjin soon returned to the skies, for it would take a major crash to ground him permanently. He and his squadron were almost out of fuel by the end of that day. He first ensured the safety

---

* All the dates here are approximate, by the way, since time was as loose a concept with him as it would be with his future wife. For example, he told everyone he was born in the first year of the Republic—1911, and that's what his headstone reads—but Nationalist Air Force records say 1915. He probably lied and said he was older than he really was just so he would be accepted, but no one knows for sure why the records say he was all of four years younger. Things pretty much disintegrate timewise from then on, and I've only been able to hazard guesses as to exactly when things happened in his life. Not that it really matters at this point. But still.

of his wounded men, even though he was running on fumes. With the sun setting directly in front of him and dusk fast approaching, J. H.'s father detected a flat area up ahead. Just as the wheels were about to touch down, he realized that he was actually descending into the treetops of an ancient forest. He ejected the moment before the plane disintegrated on impact, only to be flung through the massive canopy. Their  branches and trunks knocked out his front teeth, broke three ribs, and peeled his face from his skull as he plummeted to earth. He was airlifted over the Himalayas to a China–Burma–India Theater field hospital in Karachi, where he was somehow put back together so well that he eventually looked the same as ever. From then on he had nothing but endless praise for the American doctors who had saved his life and his handsome face, as well as the highest praise for the beautiful English nurse who had tended to him. He bought a cabochon ruby ring in India as a souvenir for his wife, but all she really remembered about this whole ordeal was his admiration for that foreign nurse.

In honor of his heroism, J. H.'s father was invited to attend the surrender of Japan's armed forces in the China Theater that was held in Nanjing on September 9, 1945, and his role was that of adjutant to the commander of the Air Force's First Military District, Chang Ting-meng. Five days later, newly promoted Combat Staff Captain Huang Longjin flew with his commander from their base in Chongqing, Sichuan, to the newly liberated island of Taiwan in order to take control of the airfields where kamikaze pilots and their aircraft were being detained. These Japanese prisoners demonstrated how the planes were operated, and the best Chinese pilot in the group was ordered to take one of the suicide planes out for a spin. J. H.'s father selected a predecessor to the infamous Zero to try out that day, and that is how he became the only Chinese pilot ever to fly a kamikaze plane.

DESPITE ALL OF HIS accomplishments, I never really knew J. H.'s father. To be honest, I don't think anyone ever did. He had learned to keep his distance from the family mêlées, resigned to his role as permanent outsider, while J. H.'s mother reinforced her primacy by insisting that her children were Northerners, that they speak Mandarin and never learn either Hakka or Cantonese. Huang Longjin could not compete for his children's love, as their showing him the slightest kindness made his wife explode. It took me a long time to parse this out, for he didn't like to talk about himself, even a little bit, and prying information out of him—even concerning his wartime exploits—required considerable patience and determination. As a result, we never had his version of his life on file, so we too often relied on our own assumptions and the spiteful whisperings of his wife to make sense of things. I tried for years to pinpoint the source of the boundless anger that surges through this family like a tangle of bad wiring, if for no other reason than that J. H. and I often found ourselves smarting from the sparking end of each manic tendril.

J. H. remembers that things weren't always this way, because it wasn't until the family was living in Beijing after the war that the marriage started to crumble. His parents never discussed this or even hinted at the reasons why J. H.'s father grew so distant. But it's not all that hard to guess. With more free time on his hands, he indulged in dancing and loose women, so his wife assumed the role of the disapproving, nagging spouse. Not that I can blame her, but this probably drove her husband even farther away, for he was brought up to believe that while women should always be chaste and obedient, men could and should take life's enjoyments where they found them. It didn't hurt that he was also unadulterated catnip with the ladies.

Since other Huang men had multiple families, it most likely seemed natural to him that he should too, so one day he put a scheme into action that would finally free him up enough for that new wife he had planned. He announced to his children's mother that while he stayed behind in Beijing, she and the children were going to sail down to Guangdong Province and then travel overland to live with his parents in their rural Hakka village. He put a malleable younger brother in charge of ensuring that the wife and kids were strong-armed onto a ship harbored in Tianjin and then transported overland to Laolong. J. H.'s mother was unable to do much about this scheme, for she had nowhere else to go and no money to live on. His plans were foiled, however, when a storm first delayed the journey and then when Little Three ran a fever. The captain refused to let a sick child on board, so the ship sailed off without them. J. H.'s mother used this reprieve to talk her way out of her husband's plans to get rid of them.

The thought of what might have happened if there had been no storm and if Little Three had not fallen ill makes me shiver. His mother would have been a prisoner in a place where she knew no one, possessed no money, and didn't even speak the language. She would have been at the mercy of strangers. She would have had to submit to the absolute authority of her husband's parents. And a few years later, when her in-laws were hauled before that firing squad, she and her little children undoubtedly would have been forced to join them.

And his father would have been free to dance and love and start again.

And all of this family's bubbling anger suddenly makes a whole lot of sense.

J. H.'s FATHER CAREFULLY arranges a finished piece next to the others and slowly picks up a new triangle. I silently start to time him:

five minutes to fill each one, and they still have to be dusted with cornstarch, fried, and then slowly braised. And this is just the first dish of many. We'll never make it at this pace, and our ravenous clan will soon be banging on his door.

"*Dàjiā jǐdiǎnzhōng lái?*" I ask, already knowing when everyone will arrive. He slowly turns toward the clock on his stove, adjusts his bifocals, and says softly in Chinese, "In three hours." I look over the rest of the ingredients for the huge meal in progress and feel the first flickers of panic. He patiently returns to the task in front of him while my eyes take in his spotted hands, which tremble slightly as he tries to coax the memory of his mother's cooking out of them. Ever since the last series of small strokes, he has lost his natural grace, the dancer's movements that were once the toast of Shanghai. Gone is the handsome tango partner and dashing fighter pilot who once dazzled the city's fallen women in wartime dance halls along the Bund. I tell myself that he's an old man, that I must be patient, that I should just learn to breathe and relax as I watch him redo all of my efforts. Suppressing my desire to take over the kitchen, I try my best to transform myself into something on the order of a submissive daughter-in-law, but my right eye twitches violently.

I finally give up and just let him work at his own pace while I settle into washing the vegetables and rice, scaling and prepping a fish, tidying the fridge and bathroom, wiping down counters, and setting out a rickety assortment of borrowed folding chairs around his table on this eve of the Year of the Monkey. My hands stay busy while my eyes keep track of how he makes the family's favorite holiday dish. I surreptitiously allow my glances to wander up his arms to his shoulders and then to the back of his head, his stiff black hair much grayer than it was only last year.

We have never gotten to know each other much beyond these kitchen encounters because Chinese tradition forbids anything other than minimal interaction between a man and his daughter-in-law (wannabe or not), meaning that he almost never even acknowledges my presence beyond what simple courtesy requires. Once he realized that I wasn't going anywhere, he was kind enough to tell J. H. that— unlike his wife and daughters—he fully accepted me as his new daughter-in-law, even though we weren't married. However, instead of drawing him closer, this newfound status has put me at an even greater distance, for propriety demands we never chat, never share ideas or thoughts, and never even look each other in the eye. I was told to call him *Bófù,* or Elder Paternal Uncle, but since we rarely speak, I seldom call him anything at all. He usually signals that he wants my attention by clearing his throat or saying the Chinese version of "Uh," at which point I raise my head and eyebrows, give him a brief nod, and traipse after him into the kitchen.

Lack of things to say has not deterred us from spending precious time together simply because we both like to cook. He teaches me his cherished recipes, the ones no one else cares to learn, the foods his ancestors probably enjoyed for generations upon generations. We both are also quietly aware that hiding by a stove allows us to maintain a Swiss-like neutrality in this family's never-ending internecine warfare. Like me, he has no dog in these fights. Bowing out of whatever fracas is taking place, we find our refuge in the kitchen, with the loudly whirring stove fan and our whacking knives creating a bell jar that deflects all discord.

His home readied for the rest of the family's imminent arrival, I arrange some plum blossoms and forsythia in an old glass jar and center it on the dining table. Chopsticks and soup spoons are placed at each setting. I sneak a peek at my boyfriend's father calmly working on the bean curd, oblivious to everything but the preparation of this one dish. My pulse slows as I remember that this kitchen of his has become my safe haven, a place where I can screen myself behind the pots and pretend I am being appropriately dutiful.

Pausing on the kitchen threshold, I see for the first time the wisdom of his measured pace. His unhurried tempo advises me that dinner will have to be presented gradually over several leisurely hours, that the cook and his helper will need to be regretfully absent from the festivities as they tend to woks and steamers, and that they will then have to spend an inordinate amount of time meticulously cleaning up the kitchen in order to guarantee good luck in the new year. With the clanging of steel and the banging of china drowning out all attempts at conversation, they will emerge sweaty and unscathed only when everyone has left. As the cool night air seeps in through the living room window and traffic noises are reduced to the occasional honk, these two will only then sit down at the cluttered table and contentedly nibble on leftovers while the eldest son tidies the apartment and returns the borrowed chairs.

I wash up, take a sip of tea, and put on a clean apron. My hand reaches for a bean curd triangle, and I hum softly to myself as I sedately scrape out a little crater. I tamp the edges of our bell jar down securely around us. We will not share another word the entire evening, but there will be no need for chitchat.

After five minutes, J. H.'s father looks over his glasses at the perfectly hollowed-out piece in my fingers and rewards me with the slightest of nods.

The Year of the Ram fades as the shadows on his desk lengthen. I pour him a fresh glass of hot jasmine tea.

There is no hurry.

IT'S A COLD WINTER morning in early January 1996. Services for J. H.'s father are being held in a few hours, so we are rushing across town from our hotel in Whittier to a shop in the San Gabriel Valley that sells nothing but Chinese funerary supplies. We will then need to hightail it twenty miles westward to downtown Chinatown during the morning rush hour in order to give his father's caregiver a lift before circling back across eastern LA County for the funeral. We don't have nearly enough time for all of this, and we know that J. H.'s mother will have a major meltdown if we are late. I compulsively check my watch, gulp down coffee, and violate all sorts of vehicle codes as I tear up Rosemead Boulevard.

We arrived in Los Angeles the morning after his passing and immediately met with the family at a mortuary. By that time, his father had already been set up in a viewing room. But instead of looking dead, he simply appeared sound asleep. That gave us no small amount of comfort, for his astounding ability to sleep through absolutely anything had been so unparalleled that we hoped he was bypassing death itself via a very long snooze. He gained world-class napper fame during a stay at Little Three's surburban house on the outskirts of Long Beach, where he busied himself tending her roses, cooking, and watching television. One day I heard on the radio that a plane had crashed into a residential part of Cerritos and that many people had been killed on the ground. Frantic, I called Little Three's home again and again, but no one answered. Many hours later, I finally got a sheriff's deputy to tell me where exactly the plane had fallen and found out it was half a mile from her home, meaning that everyone in the family was safe. When Little Three called us back that evening, she told us their father had slept through it all: crash, explosions, earthquake-level heavings of the earth, sirens, the whole enchilada. He had been peacefully and utterly oblivious.

But he wanted to have more of a social life than suburban Cerritos offered, so his final home had been in a senior citizens' highrise in LA's Chinatown. He seemed to revel in his freedom there, taking painting classes and providing female schoolmates with rides in the old VW Rabbit we had given him. Strokes had stiffened him so much that he peppered the car's interior with fish-eye mirrors. Sitting in the front of his car was like looking through the eye of a housefly. But he made it work, for he was always out and about, happily chauffeuring the ladies here and there. In English, we say that a leopard never changes its spots, but as his wife mordantly commented, "*Gǒu gǎibùliǎo chī shǐ*"—"You can't stop a dog from eating shit."

INTERSTATE 10 IS BACKED UP solid with traffic, even though the sun has barely inched over the horizon, so we continue to work our way across a network of familiar back roads to pick up everything that has been ordered for the traditional funeral planned for J. H.'s father. These items have nothing to do with Daoism or Buddhism per se, but they're necessary when seeing off the family members in this clan: bundles of sandalwood incense, red candles, piles upon piles of fake money, imitation sheets of gold and silver, red paper with lots of characters printed on them, yellow strips covered in magical script, paper clothes and other belongings, two life-size servants—one male and one female—made out of paper, and a red metal container to burn all of these things so that J. H.'s father will be comfortable and well-off in the next world. We carefully buckle the two servants in their old-fashioned garb into the middle row of our van to keep them from getting crushed, and they seem to be happy to be out for this ride. After they have been secured, we try to find room for the remaining mountain of stuff, since the back of the van is already half-filled with tangerines, apples, cookies, snacks, and every sort of candy J. H.'s father loved during his lifetime—especially the black sesame candy

wafers he enjoyed every day—and we argue and shove until the door is finally squeezed shut.

Once we've made it to Chinatown and back, we hike up the stairs toward Hsi Lai Temple in Hacienda Heights, a haze of incense guiding us toward the chants coming from Bodhisattva Hall, where three golden Buddhas—past, present, and future—bless us from their perches. All around them are walls and columns covered with tiny golden lights illuminating the even tinier names of the dead who will have prayers wash over them for, if not all eternity, then at least until the San Andreas Fault decides to rearrange the temple. Before going in, J. H. and I pause outside by the big bronze censer and look upward. We grab each other's hands and gasp at what looks like ten cranes flying toward the west, in the direction of what is called the Land of Final Happiness. The thing is, Southern California doesn't have cranes, so we take this strange vision as J. H.'s dad's way of telling us in a very lyrical way not to worry. Comforted and calm, we enter the hall and join his family as they kneel down and intone the sutras.

J. H.'s father was not a Buddhist—he never bothered to mention what it was he believed in—so we are attempting to cover all the bases. His widow is purportedly a Christian, but that doesn't matter, for it has been decided by someone or other that our first step will be this Buddhist service. After that, we head out to a small hall near the gravesite to say our good-byes. J. H.'s father has been dressed in a traditional indigo silk gentleman's gown, as no one could find his old Air Force uniform. Just before the funeral director closes his casket, his Christian second daughter slips a Bible into his hand and hooks a small cross onto a buttonhole, another bit of insurance for the long ride. She has asked a minister to say a few words, and then the Buddhist priests take over.

After their father has been lowered into the ground, we set out all of his favorite foods, weep, and kowtow to him. We array the rest of the offerings at the gravesite and spend more than an hour burning that mountain of paper and his two combustible servants, poking at the ashes with skewers now and then to ensure nothing is left behind in our red metal firebox.

Crows gather in the trees as we work, cawing loudly to their friends to join them in a noisy picnic as soon as we leave.

Black Sesame Candy Wafers (V)

HĒIZHĪMÁ TÁNG 黑芝麻糖

J. H.'s father munched on a couple of pieces of this, his favorite candy, every day, allegedly to keep his hair black but also because he had the biggest sweet tooth I've ever seen. Any trip to a Chinatown market would involve him slipping a packet of these crisp wafers into his shopping basket with a satisfied smile. They would then be opened that same afternoon when he sat down to enjoy his cup of hot jasmine tea and toasted pumpkin seeds. All of these had therapeutic value, he would inevitably assure us as he happily nibbled away. It took little encouragement for me to join in.

Even now, when we visit his grave in Southern California, we always bring him a gift of these candies, along with flowers, fruit, and cookies. Some things are just too good to let a little thing like death get in the way.

¾ cup | 100 g toasted black sesame seeds
3 tablespoons packed | 40 g black or dark brown sugar
¼ teaspoon fine sea salt
1 tablespoon honey
1 tablespoon water
1 tablespoon butter (salted or unsalted)

Line a baking sheet with a Silpat or sheet of parchment paper, and set out a rolling pin and silicone spatula, as well as a small bowl filled with boiling water. Have one more Silpat or sheet of parchment paper ready as well.

If you haven't toasted the sesame seeds yet, do so now, following the directions on page 272. Stir the sugar, fine sea salt, honey, and water in a small (1-quart | 2-liter) steel saucepan and bring to a full boil over medium heat. As soon as the top of the liquid is almost covered with bubbles, set your timer for 2 minutes. Don't stir the candy, just let it bubble away. As soon as the 2 minutes are up (or, if you're relying on a candy thermometer, it should read "hard crack," which is about 300°F | 150°C), immediately remove the pan from the heat and use a silicone spatula to stir in first the butter and then the sesame seeds, so that they become evenly coated with the candy. The mixture will turn into a soft mass that will come away from the sides of the pan.

Scrape the hot sesame candy onto the lined baking sheet. Use your silicone spatula, dipping it in the hot water as needed, to quickly turn the candy into as thin a layer as possible. Then cover it with that other sheet of Silpat or parchment paper and use the rolling pin to flatten the candy into a very thin sheet; about ¹⁄₁₆ inch | 1.5 mm is ideal, as this helps make the candy shatteringly crisp. (A good way to guesstimate is to make sure the sheet is no more than 4 or 5 seeds thick.) As soon as you have achieved the correct thickness, flip the candy out onto a cutting board while it is still warm. Use a long, heavy sharp knife to trim off the uneven edges and then cut it into rectangles. Any size is fine, but I like the shape that reminds me of the ones J. H.'s father would buy: about ¾ by 1½ inches | 20 by 40 mm. (If the weather is humid on the day you make this, refrigerate the candy in order to crisp it up.)

Cool the candy completely, then store it in a tightly closed container. I tend to keep it hidden in the refrigerator with something like *anchovies* written on the side to keep it from disappearing too quickly. *Makes about 6 ounces | 180 grams.*

Long-Bean Wreaths

DÒUJIĂO YÚRÒU JUĂN 豆角魚肉圈

Without a doubt the most beautiful recipe the Hakka people have ever invented, this also shows how frugal a dish can be in the right hands, for only a small amount of fish ends up serving half a dozen diners.

BEANS

> 12 long beans, as young and tender as possible
>
> 1 teaspoon fine sea salt

FILLING

> 12 ounces | 300 g white-fleshed fish fillets, defrosted if frozen
>
> 6 dried black mushrooms, plumped in cool water overnight (you will use 3 for the filling and 3 for the sauce; reserve the soaking liquid for the sauce, if desired)
>
> 1 square (1 inch | 2 cm wide) cured tangerine peel
>
> 2 teaspoons ice water
>
> ½ teaspoon fine sea salt
>
> ½ teaspoon sugar
>
> Freshly ground black pepper
>
> 2 green onions, finely chopped
>
> Potato starch or cornstarch for coating
>
> Peanut or vegetable oil for frying

2 tablespoons toasted sesame oil

1 tablespoon finely minced fresh ginger

The 3 sliced black mushrooms from above

½ cup | 125 ml rice wine or strained reserved mushroom-soaking
liquid

½ cup | 125 ml water

2 teaspoons regular Chinese soy sauce

1 teaspoon sugar

Finely chopped cilantro or green onions for garnish

Trim off the stem ends of the long beans. Bring a wide pan of water
to a boil and sprinkle in the fine sea salt. Add the long beans
and blanch them only until they turn bright green,
then drain in a colander set in the sink. Rinse the
beans to cool them and stop them from cooking
any further. Drain the beans and pat dry.

Wind each bean around itself into a 2-inch
| 5-cm nest and tuck the end inside to secure it.
(This is much easier than it sounds.)

To make the filling, set the fish on a couple
of layers of paper towels to absorb excess moisture while you prepare the rest of the ingredients.
Remove and discard the mushroom stems and
finely chop 3 of the caps. (Slice the other 3 caps into
strips and set them and the soaking liquid, if you
reserved it, aside for the sauce.)

Cover the tangerine peel with boiling water and

let stand for at least 10 minutes. Drain, discarding the soaking liquid, and finely mince the softened peel.

Remove any bones still hiding in the fish by pulling them out with heavy tweezers or needle-nose pliers. Cut the fish into small pieces and place in a food processor along with the tangerine peel. Whiz the fish until it clumps up into a pasty ball. Add the ice water and fine sea salt and pulse a bit more. Pulse in the finely chopped mushrooms, sugar, pepper, and green onions. You should end up with a firm, bouncy, light-green paste.

To stuff and fry the wreaths, wet your hands and shape the fish paste into 12 balls. Stick a ball into the center of each wreath. Put a couple of tablespoons of potato starch or cornstarch in a bowl and dip the tops and bottoms of the fish balls inside the wreaths into the starch to coat. Set a frying pan over medium heat and drizzle in a few tablespoons of peanut or vegetable oil. When the oil is hot, slide in as many of the filled wreaths as will fit without crowding. Fry them, turning once, until golden on both sides, then remove to a shallow serving bowl. Repeat as necessary with the rest of the filled wreaths. Pour off the oil and wipe the pan clean with a paper towel.

To make the sauce, heat the sesame oil and ginger in the frying pan until they smell wonderful, then add the sliced mushrooms and cook until they are golden brown. Pour in the rice wine or mushroom-soaking liquid, water, soy sauce, and sugar, then add the wreaths, cover, and cook until most of the sauce has been absorbed, which will take just a few minutes. Plate the wreaths and sprinkle with the cilantro or green onions. Serve hot, with lots of steamed rice. *Serves 6.*

Chapter 10

Clarity

**TIANJIN, CHINA—EARLY TWENTIETH CENTURY
(AND THE AFTERMATH)**

Figuring out where reality began with J. H.'s family and where the fabrications took over has been difficult. Until only recently, I never knew which of their tales were false assumptions or misdirects, and how history really panned out with this espoused family of mine. But as with any story, I had to start at the beginning, so that is where I began to dig. And then, somewhere along the way, I discovered that truth can be malleable, that it can be meticulously reshaped by whoever happens to be doing the telling.

Ever since I first heard of Elder Paternal Aunt, and up until the end of her life, she had been presented—and, more important, she had presented herself—as a demi-princess, the daughter of a warlord* who worked for an even greater warlord, a woman of status and importance, a person of impeccable Han lineage. She had inculcated these ideas into her children to such an extent that they too believed themselves superior to most everyone else on the planet. As I warily sidled my way into this little clan, I was so confused by pretty much everything around me that I didn't even try to make the mismatched puzzle parts fit together—meaning that it would be decades before I dared formulate any of my questions or attempted to parse things out. I was able to fully explore the lives of J. H.'s parents only from the safe distance and clear perspective that their deaths provided. J. H. and I have by now been officially married for more than two decades† and together for more

---

* Or, depending upon who was doing the talking, a warlord's right-hand man. Questions about this invariably led to arguments, so I quickly learned to keep my mouth shut.

† After we tied the knot in a super-simple civil ceremony in San Jose, J. H. and I drove down to visit his mother. She took me aside and presented me with a large White Russian amethyst necklace and ring she had bought after the war, when they all lived up in Shenyang near Siberia. She hugged me and told me that from then on she was my mother, too. I was at last the official number-one daughter-in-law. We started to tear up, and I have to admit that might have been the greater gift.

than four. That is pretty much the entirety of my adult life, so at this point I no longer know where the edges to my being end and his begin.

Foreign though I might be, it has for some reason fallen upon me to untangle the history of these two people and their forebears. But then again, time and love ended up weaving the chronicle of my husband's family into my own story, too.

WHEN J. H.'S MOTHER told us that CliffsNotes version of her early years, the world she described sounded like it was straight out of a fairy tale.

She was the daughter of a warlord, or at least something pretty close to one—this was the explanation for her exalted status and her melodramatic rages. We would take cover from her meltdowns and later roll our eyes and share a quiet, nervous laugh. We would whisper among ourselves, "Well, what can you expect? She's you-know-who's daughter through and through." Tantrums by other family members could then by extension be excused as well, for these were the fault of genes passed down from a bellicose grandpa, rather than a simple lack of manners. We licked our wounds and blamed it all on forgivable nature, not inexcusable nurture. We gave these people a free pass to manipulate and yell with abandon because that is who they were. But the question for me was always, *Honestly now, who were they?*

Any morsels of information that I ever pried out of her were stashed away in a mental box that I kept firmly padlocked for as long as she was alive. Only later was I finally able to fill in many of the blanks, using a combination of conjecture, historical records, Google, and math. So let's start at square one. She intimated that she was Han Chinese much as American bluebloods will expect you to assume they are WASPs through and through, even though no one ever puts that into actual words or takes a blood test. That day in Long Beach, she told us she had been born in the port city of Tianjin in 1922, on the sixth day of the twelfth lunar month, to the wife of a Yunnanese commander who worked under a powerful warlord.

Before we start down that road, it must be noted that the Han are China's main ethnic group. Constituting more than ninety percent of the population, the Han have always been the accepted face of the culture, the dominant influence, and the uncontested majority. China's other ethnicities—and the nation has fifty-five recognized minorities—have usually been considered peripheral, their cultures and languages little more than ciphers. Their existence was acknowl-

edged, yes, and their lands were definitely part of China, but back then you didn't eat much of their cuisines and you most definitely didn't want your daughter to marry them.

J. H.'s maternal grandfather was from Yunnan, yet I found it strange that his mother almost never mentioned this southern province except as the place where she attended college and then got married. Yunnan literally means "South of the Clouds." Perched way down on the south-central border, Yunnan is as far from China's imperial capital as you can get in that direction, a timeless place made up mainly of rocky highlands and terraced paddies, where the foods and the culture can easily fool you into thinking you might have unwittingly crossed the border into Southeast Asia. In other words, the region is so unlike Beijing and Tianjin that big-city Northerners might be tempted to regard it as the boondocks, or maybe even another country altogether.

Elder Paternal Aunt described her father to us as someone who had worked for an even greater Yunnanese warlord, one of the local strongmen who sprang up all over the country in the early years of the twentieth century. The so-called Warlord Era—replete with warring factions and private militias—lasted about twelve years, from 1916 to 1928. China's warlords were notoriously tribal, so their cliques and armies were composed of uniform languages and ethnic backgrounds. A warlord's most important officers would therefore have spoken his language and been very much like him. These strongmen might have referred to themselves as generals and covered their chests with medals, but many were in fact thugs who had risen up through the ranks of local territorial armies, while others had started out as bandits. Few were well read or cultured.

By now, you probably have come to the realization that the nobility angle of Elder Paternal Aunt's story has flown out the window.

The third thing you need to know about J. H.'s mother is that she told him on two separate occasions late in her life that her own father had grown up in the Yunnan county of Mi'le, "and so," she added that second time, "that means I am actually from Mi'le, too." She stated that her father was the official godson, or *yìzi,* of a warlord from southern Yunnan. Try as I might, I can find no record of her father ever having lived. We have no photographs or accounts of his life, nothing other than his name and the fact that he hailed from the area around Mi'le. In spite of that, these bits of information allowed me to pull at some previously unnoticed threads.

Yunnan is about the same size as Germany, but instead of being

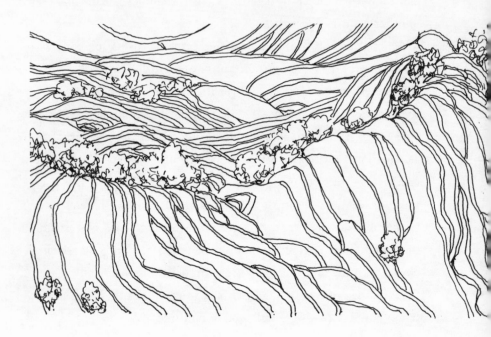

a nice, solid block like dear old Deutschland, Yunnan squiggles among the foothills of the Himalayas and loops its way into the tropical reaches of Indochina. This province is a vastly complicated place with more ethnic minorities than anywhere else in China. Mi'le, in fact, embraced the territory of a military faction that was not ethnically Han, but rather Hani, a highland tribal group that has a lot in common with the mountain people of northern Laos and Vietnam, so their food tastes more Southeast Asian than Chinese. And so, even though Elder Paternal Aunt never acknowledged this fact, her father was without a doubt Hani as well.

Chiles, rice, and corn are big deals south of Kunming and down near Yunnan's tea capital of Pu'er. Throughout the hilly country that straddles the border there with Vietnam, sour flavors, indigenous

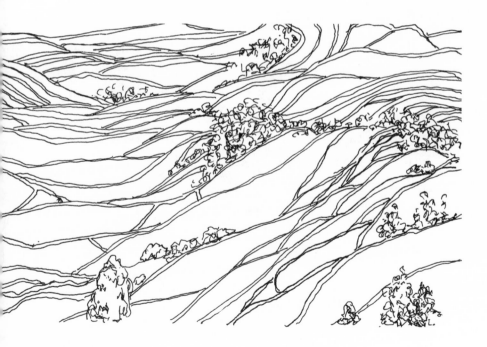

herbs, meat, coagulated blood, and bee pupae are turned into tropical meals that are anything but Han in style or flavor. Their main crop is red rice, which is grown in the thousands of stunning paddies these people have carved into the mountainsides over the past thirteen hundred years. The Hani worship the sun and the moon and fire, as well as the mountains, forests, and rivers. Both genders wear turbans, and their everyday dress is made of simple black or indigo cloth. On religious and seasonal feast days, their garb turns a riot of color, and the women ornament themselves with intricate silver jewelry.

In other words, the gap that exists between the cultures of the Han and the Hani is as enormous as the one between night and day.

THE FOURTH THING you need to know about J. H.'s mother is that her Yunnanese father somehow happened to be stationed way up north in Tianjin for only a short while. From that bit of information, and using the local history of that city as my template, I was able to pinpoint her birth year as most likely being 1919—three years before she claimed—which would have made her about kindergarten age when her world turned upside-down. While the recollections of a three-year-old would definitely be suspect six decades later, she might have been just old enough at the age of six to retain those memories of a chauffeur and all the other trappings of the good life.

So, let's say that she was born in 1919 in Tianjin to an ethnic Hani father, a certain someone who was wealthy and imposing, thanks to his close personal relationship with his warlord boss. Back then, the

Hani arranged marriages for their children when they were on the cusp of adulthood, just as the Han Chinese did. However, even more important to this tale is the fact that, unlike the Han Chinese, Hani husbands were monogamous, so they couldn't look forward to one day acquiring second or third wives. These men could, though, take on concubines back then if they were anxious to have sons and their wives could not deliver in that one department.

Which leads us to J. H.'s maternal grandmother. She has turned into one of my personal heroes, but as F. Scott Fitzgerald once wrote, "Show me a hero and I'll write you a tragedy." Liu Yukun, whom my husband's family always refers to as *Lǎolǎo*, or "Maternal Grandma," was described to us by her daughter as the official first wife of Zhou Zhongxiang, and despite my serious doubts about her status, I never questioned this out loud, as that would have been suicidal. However, all the evidence points to what was possibly a very different arrangement.

Lǎolǎo is still a beauty in the two photographs we have of her—one in happy middle age and another from late in life. Despite her good looks, she hardly possessed the sort of connections or Hani lineage a marriage broker would have been able to parlay into potential wife material for a powerful man like Zhou Zhongxiang.

Instead, the Liu family's sole claims to glory lay with two ancestors. One was a samurai named Yanagi* who settled in the northern province of Hebei near Tianjin. Family lore says that this samurai won a duel in front of a Ming emperor, so he was awarded land near Tianjin, a place that *Lǎolǎo* said was thereafter called the Village of Lord Liu, or Liu Daren Zhuang.† Her other interesting ancestor was an imperial doctor. J. H.'s mother remembered seeing the court robes he wore while attending to royal ailments, and his official carved seal was the same one she ditched during her escape from Tianjin, a story I'll touch on shortly.

Lǎolǎo was the daughter of a Han Chinese restaurateur in Tianjin. It is entirely conceivable that her father struck up some sort of friendship with the warlord's lieutenant when he came to dine. Perhaps he was a regular customer and one thing led to another, with Zhou Zhongxiang agreeing to be bound in a marriage—quasi or formal— to the restaurateur's only daughter. It's also logical to assume that this restaurateur would have gained sufficient prestige, as well as protection, from such an arrangement that he most likely would

---

* *Yanagi* in Japanese means "willow," just like the Chinese surname Liu. Elder Paternal Aunt never even heard about this ancestor, though, until she was a teenager. She was expressing her intense hatred for the Japanese over whatever new atrocity was in the paper that day when her mother looked up at her and said, "Well, there's something you should know."

† It's possible that this was renamed during the second half of the twentieth century as the more proletariat-sounding Liu Family Village, or Liujia Zhuang, for such a place can be found nestled in fields of grain around 185 miles south of Tianjin, near Hengshui.

have been willing to overlook his future son-in-law's Hani blood. Moreover, if *Lǎolǎo*'s father's finances were tight—and they most certainly were, since his death soon thereafter left his family very close to penniless—turning his daughter into a concubine rather than an official wife would have meant that he wouldn't have had to pay for either a dowry or a fancy wedding. Again, I am just extrapolating likelihoods using the available clues, but, as Sherlock Holmes famously noted, "Once you eliminate the impossible, whatever remains, no matter how improbable, must be the truth." And even if she had somehow become the official wife of Zhou Zhongxiang, her father made two big mistakes. First, the era of the warlords would be a short one. And second, he seriously underestimated his daughter.

Lǎolǎo WOULD NEVER have had any say in how her father disposed of her. She was superfluous, a mere girl. Even today, unwanted daughters are dropped off at orphanages in China to be raised, if they are lucky, by adoptive parents on the other side of the world. If they are not so lucky, they might be aborted or die soon after birth or suffer some unknown yet probably horrible fate. There is no arguing with the facts: Thirty-three million more men than women are alive now in China.

From the way *Lǎolǎo* survived later on, we know that she was highly intelligent, but she was raised to be obedient and unschooled. She couldn't even walk unassisted, since her own mother had repeatedly crushed all the bones in her feet while she was a toddler and then trussed them up so that she was left with two club-shaped monstrosities at the ends of her ankles.* And as repulsive as that barbaric tradition may have been, anyone who could mangle and stunt a little girl's feet would have had no inhibitions when it came to doing the same thing to her mind and her will. Daughters were then, as even now in many parts of China, considered burdens that would eventually belong to other families, offspring who would have to be begrudgingly fed and clothed until they finally were of marriageable age.

Yet these girls had to be given something to fill their days. And so, *Lǎolǎo*—like Elizabeth Bennet in *Pride and Prejudice*—devoted her childhood and teenage years to mastering the womanly art of embroidery. But unlike Lizzie, she never could disappear into a book and live another life inside her head, or ride a horse, or even take a walk all by herself. She was fated to be ensnared for all time in whatever ugly realities her parents and then her husband gave her. That is

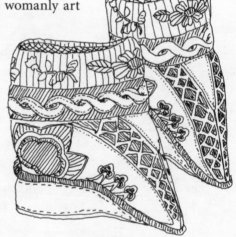

---

* Words have a way of muscling in to gag the horror of what humans do to each other while shielding the malefactors behind pleasant euphemisms. For example, Chinese men called these stumps *three-inch lotus blossoms* and once considered them erotic, while the English term *bound feet* suggests that millions upon millions of Chinese girls simply had their toes swaddled up like a ballerina's.

why, while still a child, *Lǎolǎo* was made to sew in one room while her three brothers were taught to read in another. The second of four children, she tried to listen in and learn, but she was punished whenever she was caught. All she was allowed to study, her daughter later told us, were ways to be as alluringly ladylike and feminine as possible, and ignorance was deemed sufficiently ladylike and feminine.

She passed her days as if time itself had stopped. Nothing changed until her father told her who would take her away and fulfill her destiny. She was delivered, for better or for worse, into the hands of a complete stranger and into a household where she knew no one. She was designed by her own family to be a toy that didn't talk back, one that would gradually morph into a bearer of sons. The problem is, *Lǎolǎo* failed on that last account.

It must be devastating to know that your mere arrival in this world was a grave disappointment to your family. Elder Paternal Aunt certainly felt that, since she was supposed to have been a boy. Her own mother's fortunes would have improved considerably if that had happened, for her father would not have abandoned them. But then again, if she had been born a boy, chances are very good that her father would have sent this child back to his home village to be raised properly: as a Hani, as his heir, as proof of his manhood. *Lǎolǎo* would, as in all things, have had no say in the matter. Despite this unspoken fact, Elder Paternal Aunt, over the years that I knew her, would occasionally sink into deep depressions that made her mourn aloud the curse of having been born a girl. It was because of her gender that her father never returned, that her own mother was left without support, and that her younger uncles were cut loose from all that had sustained them.

Ah, the uncles. *Lǎolǎo*'s eldest brother was an English interpreter in Tianjin's British foreign concession, one of the many extraterritorial lands China had been forced to cede to Western countries and Japan following the Opium Wars in the mid-1800s. He lorded this job over the rest of his family, for he had a steady income, could walk where other Chinese were forbidden to tread, and was an indispensable tool for his Anglo overlords. His wife marginalized her in-laws and did her best to ensure that everyone understood her husband was the family's sole success story. This older brother interacted with his family less and less as time went on, particularly after the assassination of Zhou Zhongxiang cut them loose from any tenuous connections to power or money. The youngest brother didn't do much, never married, and was mainly dependent on his sister, while the middle brother drifted through life, unstable and fragile, and hanged himself in despair when their mother died.

And that left *Lǎolǎo* to keep the family going. Even after their world crashed around them, she found a way to manage a shipping warehouse and make certain that her mother and brothers were taken care of, that her only child was educated and well loved. *Lǎolǎo*'s decision to allow her daughter to have normal feet enabled J. H.'s mother to join other girl students in an organized escape just as the Japanese were poised to invade Tianjin in 1937. Japan's soldiers were notorious for their almost inhuman savagery—especially toward women—so while the city was preparing itself for a siege and bombardment, and then the inevitable horrors and humiliations of a long occupation, these girls slipped away on a long journey to Yunnan.

The one thing Elder Paternal Aunt remembered from the day she headed out occurred when she was about to embark on the ship in Tianjin's harbor and was standing in line for the gangway. Up ahead she could see official-looking men rummaging through the passengers' luggage. She had little of value with her, just the carved jade seal of that ancestor who had served as an imperial physician. When she was getting ready to leave Tianjin, perhaps forever, her mother had wanted to give her something small and precious of her own, a little bit of her ancestral history to carry with her throughout the rest of her life, so it was wrapped up and stuffed away in her baggage. But standing there, unsure of who was inspecting the luggage and what would happen if the seal were discovered, the girl panicked and slid it to one of her schoolmates to hide. And that was the last she ever saw of that priceless heirloom.

J. H.'s mother never talked much about that journey. Instead, she glossed over it when she described her escape: "We sailed from Tianjin to Annam"—the old name for Vietnam—"and we then walked all the way to Kunming." That's the sum of what she told us. But this doesn't tell even half of the story. From what I've been able to piece together using the records of other evacuees, she and her fellow students would have sailed down the dangerous, rocky coastline through Shanghai and Hong Kong. From there, the ship would have headed out for China's southernmost province, the island of Hainan, before crossing the South China Sea and docking in Haiphong in northern Vietnam. Then she probably took a two-week boat trip up the Red River through Hanoi, all the way to the town of Manhao in southern Yunnan. After that, she would have had to hike two hundred miles overland through the mountain ranges that ring the southern edge of the province to its capital of Kunming.

These lands are mainly populated by two of Yunnan's main minorities, the Hani and the Yi, so she would have, strangely enough, most likely passed near her father's home in Mi'le and through lands controlled by her late father's boss. But the trip, though arduous, would also have been stunning. Down in that area, the undulating peaks of the Ailao Mountains in Yuanyang County are so blanketed with intricately carved rice paddies that the ancient terraces have been designated a UNESCO World Heritage Site: the Honghe Hani Rice Terraces.

Elder Paternal Aunt had to work in order to survive, and she did this in addition to her full-time studies at National Southwest Associated University in Kunming. Her job was a good one, for she was the assistant to the dean of the university's famous medical school, Huang Rongzeng. She must have greatly impressed her employer, because he eventually introduced her to his younger cousin, the dashing Huang Longjin. This still boyish-looking fighter pilot immediately fell for the northern beauty and pursued her, not with candy and flowers—this was wartime Yunnan, remember—but with sweet potatoes. On their frequent dates, he would peel the raw tubers for her and they'd eat them like carrots while she sat in an old temple and did her homework.

Living on her own among strangers in south-central China granted her opportunities to remake herself and rewrite her own life story, and so she did. Some were little white lies, a smattering of inconsequential fibs meant to boost her perceived value, as when she told her boyfriend that she could play the piano, which she definitely could not. But she was not likely the youthful eighteen years old that she claimed when she was married—more probably twenty-one and veering very close to what was then considered "old maid" territory. She possibly informed her future husband that she was the daughter of a warlord, when her father was merely a warlord's lieutenant. And she doubtless kept silent on the fact that she was half Hani, not a pure-blooded Han. But if *Lǎolǎo* had indeed been a concubine, this was probably something that her daughter might have never known.

J. H. MET HIS maternal grandmother for the first and only time during the summer of 1946, when she came to stay with them in Beijing for a fortnight. Even though the final throes of the country's civil war still rumbled on the horizon, his parents were enjoying their first peaceful summer in more than a decade. The Huangs moved into a dark house just a few blocks west of the former imperial gardens. While his father went to work in a building on the royal estate, J. H. amused himself by playing in an area that only a few decades earlier had been off limits to all but the highest born. This corner of the gardens was later walled off and turned into official residences for China's leaders following the proletariat revolution of 1949, but that was in the future. Nationalist China still had a small handful of years to go.

Lǎolǎo met her son-in-law and three grandchildren soon after Little Three was born. Upon being introduced to her first grandson, she gently rubbed J. H.'s shaven head and found two small bumps, which she said were auspicious, as they resembled the sprouting horns of a dragon. Since his family nickname was Little Dragon, this was well and good. Not long after her arrival, she changed into a beautiful traditional dress and took her grandson shopping at nearby Xidan Market. There his grandmother granted all of his wishes—all, that is, except for a shiny sword he coveted. She tried to distract him with the sweets he loved, like *tánghúlú*, which are fresh hawthorns— a northern fruit that looks a bit like a crabapple but with a sandy texture—threaded on a stick and covered with a hard syrup. The glasslike shell crunched as he enjoyed his treat, but nevertheless he remained vaguely disgruntled, as would any five-year-old boy who ever had been denied the fun of wielding a deadly weapon.

What is truly strange, though, is that *Lǎolǎo* was not invited to be a regular visitor. In fact, she never saw her grandchildren or her son-in-law again.

This might have had something to do with the disintegration of J. H.'s parents' relationship in Beijing, for that is when his father tried to exile his first family to Laolong so that he could marry a young lady named Miss Kang.* Perhaps he was too occupied with his own dalliances to deal with his wife's mother. Perhaps he was afraid his mother-in-law would try to move in as a live-in nanny—the normal role Chinese widowed grandmothers adopt—but that would have shored up his wife's side in the balance of power, and his mother-in-law definitely would have had something to say about Miss Kang and that planned deportation. Perhaps it was something simpler, and he believed that his mother-in-law was bad luck, since two husbands had died on her. Perhaps it was because she was living as a widow with her second husband's children and now belonged to another family. Perhaps he was ashamed that his mother-in-law had remarried at all, for so-called "chastity arches" had been built in years gone by—by hard-hearted male elders, of course—to commemorate the widows they deemed virtuous, women who lived and died in absolute purdah and poverty.† It could have

* When J. H.'s tongue-tied father attempted to explain his girlfriend's attributes to his wife, the most that he could manage to blurt out was that Miss Kang was from a good family who had a five-pound thermos. Why this vacuum-insulated bottle was so important and why it was described in terms of poundage rather than volume has never, to my knowledge, been explained to anyone's satisfaction.

† As the Song dynasty neo-Confucianist Cheng Yi famously intoned about these

been all of these, or it could have been something else altogether. We simply don't know.

But then the situation became even weirder. Not too long after his grandmother's visit, J. H., his mother, and his two siblings went on an overnight trip to Tianjin. His mother said she had some business to attend to there—she never said what—but the children didn't get to stay with or even see their grandmother. Instead, they slept in a small house that belonged to *Lǎolǎo* and were tended to by the nanny their grandmother had thoughtfully provided. J. H.'s youngest great-uncle showed up that day and treated the boy to a short jaunt outside to buy sugarcane, but that was the total sum of J. H.'s relationship with any of his mother's relatives. They then returned to Beijing, and apart from a few phone calls his mother placed before J. H.'s family left for Taiwan, *Lǎolǎo* disappeared from their lives forever.

Many years later, Elder Paternal Aunt learned that Mr. Zhang's children had come to love her mother like their own. When times were bad and her stepchildren desperately needed money, she sold the one thing she had left from the old days—a precious imperial-

---

unfortunate women: "Starvation is not important, [but] the loss of chastity is."

green jade bracelet—and gave the proceeds to them. *Lǎolǎo* was selfless to the very end.

THE LIVES AND THE CHOICES all these people made began to make sense to me only when I view them through this fractured prism. I would give a lot to be able to sit down with J. H.'s parents and ask them whether I guessed right, to have them correct any misunderstandings and fill in all of those pesky blanks. But then again, they would probably be as close-lipped now as they ever were.

As I write, next to me sits a faded black-and-white portrait of *Lǎolǎo*, this extraordinarily beautiful woman I never met, but someone I nevertheless feel that I know so well. Surely this is because her face reminds me so much of my husband's. Her photograph is undated, and we don't know the occasion for this formal picture, yet a dark slick of lipstick and a subtle smile in her eyes and at the corners of her mouth suggest this was taken at the time of her marriage to Mr. Zhang. Her gaze is calm, strong, and intelligent. Her thick black hair is smoothed back toward her nape, exposing a high forehead and the straight hairline of a samurai great-great-something grandfather. Her youngest grandson inherited her faintly mismatched roundish eyes, while my husband bears the same forehead, as well as her eyebrows, nose, and jawline.

I place a small vase of narcissus and some tangerines in front of her as a small offering. I hope she found happiness for a few precious years surrounded by people who loved and honored her. Many years later, her youngest grandson relocated her ashes to a small, tree-covered island in the Lotus Blossom Sea, down near Ningbo in Zhejiang Province. Putuo Shan is one of the four sacred mountains in Chinese Buddhism, so in the end *Lǎolǎo* was given a hallowed place to look out on the sea forever and maybe find the peace that life never managed to give her.

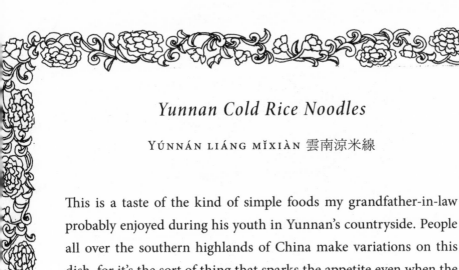

Yunnan Cold Rice Noodles

YÚNNÁN LIÁNG MǏXIÀN 雲南涼米線

This is a taste of the kind of simple foods my grandfather-in-law probably enjoyed during his youth in Yunnan's countryside. People all over the southern highlands of China make variations on this dish, for it's the sort of thing that sparks the appetite even when the weather is hot and muggy. This is traditionally made with Zhaotong chile paste, but because that is—at least for the present—impossible to find, I've come up with a really great substitute: Korea's *gochujang* paste mixed with Sichuan peppercorns and peanuts. Add more of the *gochujang* paste if you'd like the dish zippier.

About 1 pound | 500 g dried round rice noodles (*see* Tips)

2 tablespoons plus 1 teaspoon peanut or vegetable oil

8 ounces | 200 g soybean sprouts or 4 ounces | 100 g mung bean sprouts

8 ounces | 250 g ground pork

3 to 4 cloves garlic, chopped

2 to 3 tablespoons *gochujang* paste (*see* headnote), or to taste

½ cup | 40 g chopped garlic chives (*see* Tips)

1 teaspoon toasted ground Sichuan peppercorns, or to taste

¼ cup (or more, if you like) finely chopped toasted peanuts

2 to 3 tablespoons sweet soy sauce, or 2 tablespoons regular

Chinese soy sauce plus 1 teaspoon sugar

2 tablespoons rice vinegar

1 tablespoon balsamic vinegar

1 teaspoon regular Chinese soy sauce

½ cup | 20 g coarsely chopped cilantro

Bring about 4 cups | 1 liter water to a boil in a saucepan. Add the rice noodles and stir. As they soften, work them apart with chopsticks or tongs so that they don't form clumps. The noodles should be cooked, like any pasta, just to the point of al dente and no more, as this gives them personality. (Check the package directions, as each brand of rice noodles is different.) When the noodles are plump and fully hydrated, dump them into a colander set in the sink, then rinse under cool water to stop the cooking. Transfer the noodles to a bowl and toss with 1 teaspoon of the oil to keep them from sticking together as they cool down.

Bring a saucepan of water back to a full boil. Meanwhile, check over the sprouts and discard any discolored ones, as well as any loose seed coats. Add the sprouts to the boiling water. If using soybean sprouts, cook them until the yellow heads no longer taste raw but retain a nice crispness, about 10 minutes. Mung bean sprouts only need to be blanched briefly. Drain the sprouts in a colander and rinse under cool water to stop the cooking. Add to the rice noodles and toss.

Set a wok over medium-high heat. Add the remaining 2 tablespoons oil, swirl it around, and then add the pork, breaking it up into smaller clumps as you go. Add the garlic and stir-fry the meat for a few minutes until it is no longer pink. Add the *gochujang* paste and toss for about 30 seconds to coat the meat.

Add the pork to the rice noodles, along with the chopped chives, toasted ground Sichuan peppercorns, and peanuts. Then toss the noodle mixture with the sweet soy sauce (or sweetened soy), both vinegars, regular soy sauce, and cilantro, and divide the noodles among four bowls. Taste and adjust the seasoning. Serve immediately, while the vegetables are still vibrant. *Serves 4.*

Tips
Hollow, Jiangxi-style dried rice noodles (called *làifěn*) work especially well here. Whatever noodles you choose, make sure they are about the thickness of spaghetti to give them enough heft to hold their own against the rest of the ingredients. Because they are also hollow, Italian *bucatini*, though made out of wheat instead of rice, are a good substitute.

If you can't find garlic chives in your area, finely dice an equivalent amount of the green parts of green onions and add a minced clove of garlic.

Caramelized Garlic Fish

SUÀNBÀR YÚ 蒜瓣兒魚

This is something Elder Paternal Aunt used to love: little fish braised with lots of garlic. She used to call this type of cooking *ngao* in her native Tianjin dialect, but in Mandarin it is simply *āo*, which means "braised." This was true home cooking, as far as she was concerned, and yet it was something she rarely got to eat until I figured out how to make it.

Consider this a study in balance. There is just enough salt, vinegar, sugar, and oil to form perfect harmony. The vinegar is especially important, because it tempers the fishiness of this Northern dish. The caramelized sugar then cuts the tartness, the salt wakes up the taste buds, and the oil mellows everything out. Lots of garlic is called for too, but because it is cooked so slowly, its natural pungency is transformed into a gentle sweetness.

Traditionally, this recipe calls for small yellow croakers, which you often can find in the frozen section of Korean and Chinese supermarkets and which usually have their heads and most of their bones already removed. Slightly similar fish, such as porgy, mullet, and whiting, can be substituted, as long as they are not too small and delicate. (Or, if you prefer, use a filet of halibut or some other mild, firm fish—just cook and serve it whole so that the fish doesn't disintegrate.) Leave the bones in the fish or remove them—whatever you prefer; just be sure they are gutted and the gills are removed. If you're not feeding children or others who might have trouble with the bones, try them bone-in, the Chinese way. It's fun to nibble your way through dinner.

Around 7 ounces | 200 g frozen small yellow croakers, defrosted
    (*see* headnote)
10 cloves garlic, peeled (*see* Garlic Roast Chicken, page 91, for an
    easy way to peel garlic)
3 green onions
3 tablespoons peanut or vegetable oil
3 tablespoons Shaoxing rice wine
2 tablespoons water
2 tablespoons light rice vinegar
1 tablespoon regular Chinese soy sauce
3 tablespoons sugar
½ teaspoon fine sea salt

Rinse the fish, then wrap them in paper towels and gently squeeze out the water. Let them drain on a dry paper towel while you prepare the rest of the ingredients. (If you're using fresh fish, skip this step.) You can also remove the bones at this point.

Thinly slice the garlic. Cut off the white parts of the green onions and slice into ½-inch | 1 cm pieces. Slice the greens on an angle into 1-inch | 2 cm pieces.

Heat the oil in a large frying pan over medium-high until the oil is hot. Carefully add the fish to the hot oil (this way, they shouldn't stick to the pan), lightly shake the pan to keep the fish loose, and adjust the heat so that the fish brown gently. Once they are browned on the first side, carefully turn them over with a spatula, add the sliced garlic and the whites of the green onions, and gently shake the pan again. As soon as both sides of the fish have turned gold, pour off all but a tablespoon of the oil from the pan.

Add the rice wine, water, rice vinegar, soy sauce, sugar, and fine sea salt to the pan. Bring the liquid to a boil and allow the fish to simmer uncovered; don't stir the fish too much, so as to prevent them from falling apart, but do shake the pan now and then and poke things around with your spatula so that the fish cook evenly. When the sauce has reduced to a lovely caramel, sprinkle the onion greens on top, lower the heat, and cover the pan for a few minutes, until the greens have wilted. Serve hot or warm, with hot steamed bread (J. H.'s mom would have insisted on this) so that you can enjoy every drop of the sauce. *Serves 3 or 4.*

Chapter 11

Proficiency

CHENGDU, SICHUAN—2017

The city that sparkles below me, the one that is stirring itself awake window by window, calls to me, urging me to explore its delicious secrets. I can't smell a thing this high up, but my mouth waters at the thought of what is in store today. Wrapped in a plush hotel robe and too excited to sleep any longer, I push the heavy curtains all the way open to look out on Sichuan's capital. Chengdu is my husband's birthplace, and although this is his first time back since 1941, he is content for now to dream on the other side of the dark room. I nestle myself into a corner of the tall window, sip my coffee, and watch the rivers of lights thirty floors below slowly fade as daylight winds its way into the narrow concrete valleys.

Massive modern skyscrapers are springing up almost overnight in Sichuan's capital, but a stroll down an alley will lead you to quiet pockets that speak to the city's 2,300-year-old history, to raucous throngs of ladies in matching uniforms exuberantly performing calisthenics to pop music played at full volume, to hawkers selling dandan noodles and wontons bathed in chile oil, to the same sort of high-tech hipsters who decorate Silicon Valley. We've only been here a couple of days at the behest of the State Department to help the American Consulate in this city celebrate July Fourth, yet I'm rapidly falling in love with the people, the place, the food.

The day before yesterday, I went grocery shopping with renowned chef Lan Guijun, the owner of a restaurant so tony and exclusive that it doesn't even have a sign out front. Set inside a traditional house, Yuzhilan offers exquisite set meals much like the French Laundry in California's Napa Valley. I'm told that Chef Lan never allows anyone into his kitchen, but today he is going to make an exception. I will be his sous-chef for a few hours, thanks to my new status as a cookbook author.

THE 2016 PUBLICATION of my big book, *All Under Heaven: The 35 Cuisines of China,* the one that eventually brought me here, signaled my third big career change. I had started out, of course, interpreting in Taiwan for all those cultural institutions and translating scholarly articles and books. Then, after we returned to California in 1985, my work angled off into a slight—but nonetheless unsurprising—detour when I became a professional Mandarin interpreter for the state and federal courts.

Nothing prepares a person for fluency in another language quite as quickly as court interpreting. Words had to flow rapidly into my ears in one language while smoothly issuing out of my mouth in another. I also had to master all the terminology required to discuss any type of case that came up in the criminal, civil, family, juvenile dependency, traffic, administrative law, and appeals courts, as well as a large number of intellectual property lawsuits.

Pretty soon I was in high demand for depositions in Silicon Valley's high-tech cases, since this called for a different type of interpretation—consecutive—where the witness or attorney spoke a few sentences so that I could interpret them and the court reporter in turn could take down every word. The upside is that I was able to develop a shorthand system for my notes that allowed me to accurately translate highly technical discussions on everything from etching processes to advanced coding. But if there is one big downside to this sort of high-pressure, grueling, ten-hour-day interpreting, it is that it rewires the brain. As a result, I gradually developed a slight stutter, one that still pops up whenever I'm tired and my brain starts to switch back and forth frantically between the two languages in search of some dropped line of thought. The other problem is that I'm often unable to turn off the interpreter switch, which continues to run at high speed at all times. And so, even though it's been more than a decade since I retired from the courts, I nevertheless continue to interpret television programs on autopilot in my head, as well as conversations, billboards, tweets, movies, you name it.

WHENEVER I HAD a slow week during those busy years, or even a couple of extra hours, I spent them reading up on the cuisines of China. J. H. and I longed to eat the foods we had enjoyed so much in Taipei, but during the mid-1980s the Bay Area's Chinese grocery stores and restaurants still tended to be either Cantonese or Chinese American. Living in California meant I had to work really hard at figuring out ways to re-create such Shanghainese specialties as our beloved *pot-au-feu* and sprouted fava beans, Mr. Ye's roasted chicken legs, traditionally fermented Sichuan pickles, and a good approximation of that distant Hakka cousin's secret smoked chicken recipe.

Every visit to a Chinatown and every flight across the Pacific led

to new additions to our Chinese-language cookbook collection, and pretty soon our California kitchen counters were lined with fizzing vats and the refrigerator with freshly pickled vegetables, stashes of dried fish and crustaceans hid in the vegetable bin, jars upon jars of funky ingredients found places in the cupboards, and the garage was home to the overflow. I ended up writing *All Under Heaven* to create a lasting record of the dishes I first came to know and love in Taiwan, and later on in Mainland China and everywhere else. It offers more than three hundred recipes from every part of that vast country, and it is the first one to offer the hypothesis that China has five major culinary regions and thirty-five cuisines, and so is home to as many—if not more—food traditions as in Europe.

Even though that may sound like a lot of recipes, my first draft was even more ambitious. In fact, one could even call it a tad insane: I wrote up a proposal for a book of fifteen hundred recipes, a virtual *Larousse Gastronomique* of China's cuisines that would have given Western readers a fuller view of its incredible range and brilliance. This idea was, sad to say, not well received. In fact, I couldn't interest a single publisher in the project. My agent at the time informed me that no one was all that interested in cooking Chinese food, that it involved what was felt to be too much chopping and stir-frying and oil flying about. I begged to differ, so he suggested I check out the cookbook shelves at a local Barnes & Noble bookshop. And he was right. All the books on Asian cuisines were tucked into a small corner of one shelf, and those with titles that included such words as *Complete* and *Chinese* and *Cookbook* often were not much more than an inch thick and padded with photographs. I asked him what I should do.

"Write about Italian food," he exclaimed enthusiastically. "Everybody likes that."

For about three seconds I considered moving to Italy, learning fluent Italian, marrying an Italian, and basically starting my life over—before I woke up and decided I needed a new agent more than I needed a new husband. I then plowed through about four more agents in my increasingly desperate search for someone—anyone, really—who would accept my manuscript. In the end, I found myself without an agent, a publisher, or even a source of income, for I had retired from the courts in order to focus on this new career. In 1994, William Morrow had published J. H.'s study of Sun-tzu's *Art of War*, and that freed him up to take a new look at the *Dao De Jing*, China's earliest philosophical treatise, but the lack of a steady income from either of us meant we had to keep our expenses to a bare minimum. J. H.'s daughter was living with us by then and going to college, so we moved to a larger house on the edge of a cemetery, which ensured that only very quiet neighbors surrounded us. Apparently few people found living next to a graveyard all that alluring, so the rent for our beautiful Silicon Valley home with its stunning view of the emerald Santa Cruz Mountains was remarkably low, and this gave me just enough breathing space to figure out what to do.

A weird twist of fate caused a McSweeney's editor to contact me in search of a recipe for the Chaozhou-style beef soup known as *buk kat tay*, and pretty soon one thing led to another. Of course, at the first opportune moment I brought up my proposal for a considerably pared-down version of my book. She read it and asked me to cook a demo lunch for her and her coworkers. She liked what she ate, she offered me my first book contract, and—since she was also working at *Lucky Peach*—she then suggested I write and illustrate an article for that ground-breaking new food magazine. This article was later turned into the magazine's handout at a MAD symposium in Copenhagen, and soon thereafter into my second book, *The Dim Sum Field Guide*. All of a sudden, my third career took flight. It might all sound so easy in retrospect, but that first book ended up taking twice as long to sell as it did to write. Nevertheless, *All Under Heaven* was released in 2016 to surprisingly great reviews. It was nominated for a James Beard Award in 2017, the same year that a short story I wrote about J. H.'s mother, entitled "Good Graces," was nominated for the Beard Foundation's M. F. K. Fisher Distinguished Writing Award, which in turn planted the seed for this memoir you're reading.

And all of this led me by a very circuitous path to Chengdu.

FOR LUNCH TODAY, we are having something that in Chinese is called "garlic mud white meat," or *suànní báiròu*, and that I have rechristened as Garlic Lava Pork (page 258). I had eaten it many times before in other cities, but this version is a revelation. We run across it in a busy local restaurant after spending a long morning hunting down out-of-print books in some tiny alleys west of the Qing Yang ("Green

Goat") Temple. Our search for antique cookbooks has continued unabated, for my husband and I worry that the old ways will disappear. A small shop next to the winding Modi River manages to reward our search with some delightful finds, and so J. H. finds himself laden down with way too many heavy tote bags as we hike happily back over a bridge in search of something good to eat.

My heart takes a leap when I see the characters for Yibin on this restaurant, since that town is famous for what it calls burning noodles, or *ránmiàn*—a sort of variation on dandan noodles, but a whole lot nuttier and a whole lot less meaty. I drag J. H. by the hand as I scurry toward lunch. With a history spanning four millennia, Yibin—a city located along the southeastern edge of Sichuan near Yunnan—is ancient even by Chinese standards. The foods here have therefore had plenty of time to develop in many wonderful ways, transforming into a delectable fusion of Han Chinese and local minority (mainly Yi and Miao) cuisines. We of course get the noodles and they are predictably delicious, but that cold pork dish, which is on every table here, has been created with a good dash of culinary brilliance. On the surface, it's just poached boneless pork sliced over exquisitely slender ribbons of cucumber, but massive amounts of ever-so-slightly tamed garlic roam around in its vinaigrette. I rise from my meal with potent breath and the strong desire to eat there every day for as long as we are in Chengdu.

It's not just the restaurant dishes that beguile me here, for even the simplest street foods and snacks of this city make me crave more, always more. Almost daily, we visit different street vendors to buy bags of what are called Strange-Flavor Peanuts (page 256) and try to parse out their flavors, for I am anxious to make them once we get home. I pensively munch on a nut while holding out the latest purchase to J. H. as we wander down an alley.

"What spices do you taste?" I ask him. He closes his eyes in concentration and solemnly chews a few nuts. "What's in there besides salt and sugar and chiles and Sichuan peppercorns? Some have five-spice, but this one . . . this one's perfect. I can taste black pepper for sure, but what is that other thing?"

He takes another handful, and I think that's more because he loves peanuts as much as he loves me. Finally he says one word: *zīrán*, or cumin. Cumin always throws me because until recently it so rarely showed up in any of the foods of China I ever encountered, and my old dictionaries didn't even have an entry for the word. This spice's wonderful scent finally captured me in 2001 when we visited Xinjiang—in the breads of the Uyghur people, in their roasted lamb and vegetables, in their barbecued fish and chicken. Always toasted in China, cumin's earthy aromas jostled with chiles and garlic and oil to make aromatic rubs that sang of Central Asia. The scent of cumin perfumes the street foods of Sichuan because this province was once considered the edge of Han China, lying as it does so close to the massive areas known as Xinjiang and Qinghai that are home to many non-Han Chinese.

That first flight across the breadth of China to Ürümqi finally allowed me to comprehend the incredible size and diversity of this country, for the capital of the Xinjiang Uyghur Autonomous Region lies near the exact center of the Asian landmass. Even so, I still couldn't wrap my head around the fact that from where I stood in Xinjiang's capital, Cyprus was as distant from me as Japan, that we were farther away from the ocean than any other place on the planet. I raised my nose and smelled the air. It smelled of the desert and, yes, of cumin.

As we crisscrossed the country, that old map in my Taipei language school finally managed to take on its true colorations. Those flat pastels were replaced with a more stunning reality: dark forests, wide rivers, ocher deserts, the gray moonscape of the Gobi, the countless dry peaks of the massive Qinling Mountain Range that had erupted from the earth millions of years ago and sawed the country in half, shimmering rice paddies, towering cities, and miles upon miles stretching into the horizon. I gazed at the real China down below, and a shiver ran through me as I finally began to grasp the enormity and intense beauty of this land I'd come to love so ardently.

CHEF LAN WELCOMES US and shows us around before introducing me to his traditional way of making golden-thread noodles. He sets a large square of stiff egg dough on a smooth wooden counter and then positions a heavy bamboo pole on top of it.* One end of the pole is connected to the wall with a large swivel so that he can ride the other end, bouncing up and down on the pole and directing it back and forth to properly knead his impossibly sturdy dough. When Chef Lan deems the dough smooth enough to proceed, he rolls it out into a smooth, silky sheet that he then dusts with flour and curls up like a scroll. With great ceremony, he removes a heavy iron blade from the wall and hands it to me to admire before he shreds the dough into minuscule threads. I count fourteen cuts before each rest, at which point he moves the blade an inch down the roll. He tells me to finish it up, and he looks pleased when I also produce fourteen tiny strands before each pause.

Satisfied that I am able to follow directions to a T, he then leads us to his streamlined galley kitchen. He asks me whether I still want to help him cook, and of course I say yes, so he tells me to get ready. I feel quite nervous as I don the striped apron I have brought from home.

"Chef, what would you like me to do first?"

"Clean the mushrooms." I scrupulously clean and trim a pile of matsutake while he puts the rest of his small team to work. No

---

* Oddly enough, almost the exact same thing can be seen in Elizabeth David's 1977 masterwork, *English Bread and Yeast Cookery.*

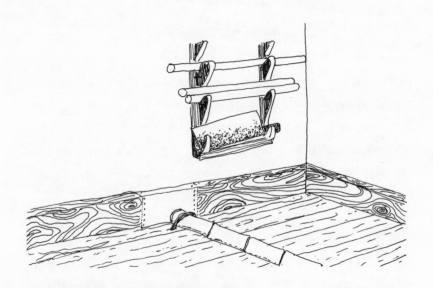

stranger to the exacting demands described by famous French and Chinese chefs, I scour my work area once I have finished with the mushrooms. I notice a little sparkle in his eye when I clean up every speck on the floor before washing and drying my hands.

"Ready to do something else?" He doesn't wait for me to answer before placing three whole carp in a dry wok. "Watch." He starts tossing the whole fish—scales, innards, fins, and all—with a wok spatula over a low flame. Toss, toss, toss. He chops them up a bit with the spatula before he hands everything over to me. "Now keep tossing them and breaking them down." Wondering whether he is doing the Chinese equivalent of giving me some crayons to play with while the adults do the real work, I settle into some serious grunt work.

"How long should I keep tossing them?" I ask. "Until I tell you to stop," he replies. He glances my way every five minutes or so to see whether I am showing any signs of flagging, but I have no intention of giving up. An hour later, the three fish have disintegrated

into a pile of dry and fluffy shreds, at which
point he tells me to stand to one side. He
pours boiling water over the flaked fish
and brings the milky liquid to a simmer before straining out the broth and
seasoning it with a sprinkle of salt. The
chef then rewards my labors with a spoonful
of the purest essence of fish I have ever tasted.
In the wrong hands, this could easily have
become strange and unappetizing. But here,
in the right hands—or at least under the
right supervision—those three fish were transformed into an intensely glorious broth.

After a short break, J. H. and I sit down with members of the
American Consulate and a few new friends to an exquisite meal in
Yuzhilan's private dining room, which is decorated like a scholar's
den replete with refined pieces of art. Each course is a delight—his
tasting menu consisting of refined riffs on Chengdu's classic dishes—
for not only are they as delicious as promised, but we are personally
served by Chef Lan himself, who explains every dish to us so that we
may properly understand and appreciate it. Just like at the French
Laundry, we are presented with only tiny morsels throughout all of
the twenty courses, meaning that fish-fragrant eggplant is transformed into two delicate slices napped with sauce, a serving of multicolored noodles with lobster eggs is artfully arranged into a precise
little disc, and a midmeal palate cleanser appears as a translucent
jelly blob with a single salted plum nestled on top. The last course is,
as at all great Chinese meals, hot soup. Strands of the most delicate

golden noodles imaginable float in a small bowl of fish broth, and, as I had a hand in making both, the chef gives me an impish smile when he sets it in front of me.

ANOTHER FRIEND IN Chengdu has introduced us to her father, a retired chef of the traditional local cuisine, and he has invited us to the family home for dinner. This day is one of the hottest days I've ever lived through, but fortunately Chef Yang welcomes us to the table with an array of cold dishes: chilled celtuce leaves drizzled with a slightly spicy nutty dressing, shredded pig ears tossed with cilantro and green onions, and crisp batons of cucumbers in a slightly tart sauce. Thoughts of the weather being too hot to eat vanish as we devour these with delight. Soon other specialties of the city arrive, like kung pao chicken, little meatballs in a clear broth studded with crystalline chunks of winter melon, and a steamed butterflied carp that is as tender as custard.

We talk as we eat, and I try to find out more about what the food of Chengdu used to be like before the Cultural Revolution, whether it has always been as *m1 mà là,* or numbing and hot, as Westerners have been led to believe. I had of course dined many times on Chengdu's *haute cuisine* in Taipei, and that exquisite meal at Yuzhilan had offered only the occasional hint of heat, but had those been outlier experiences? Chef Yang smiles and waves at the empty platters and bowls in front of us as if to say, *Judge for yourself.* And he's right. Only a few of his dishes have been even a little bit spicy; the numbing fragrance of toasted Sichuan peppercorns graced the celtuce and blackened dried chiles perfumed the kung pao chicken, but little else. His dinner was more concerned with emphasizing the inherent flavors of his perfectly fresh ingredients than in bombarding us with sensory overload. He talks about having cooked for Chairman Mao, his life in professional kitchens, and his membership in an association of retired Chengdu chefs. We ask whether we may meet them. He says he'll see, perhaps for our next visit, which is scheduled for September. And sure enough, a few months later J. H. and I find ourselves facing a round table of about thirty older men who are not quite sure what to make of my theory that China has more than eight great cuisines.

I really can't blame them. Up until only about a hundred years ago, China merely categorized its foods and cultures and people as being from either the North or the South, with the Chang Jiang as their general demarcation line. Nowadays most Chinese epicures will assure you their country has a small family of great gastronomies. Some will men-

tion as few as four, but rarely does anyone posit more than ten, with the usual number tending to be eight. At first glance, this does seem to present an extraordinarily easy way of grasping China's incredibly complex food culture, but few people ever stop to consider why only Shandong, Jiangsu, Zhejiang, Anhui, Fujian, Guangdong, Sichuan, and Hunan provinces make the grade. Over the past forty years, I've never heard of anyone worrying whether or not this notion has any factual basis, what it means both culturally and gastronomically to be excluded, and what the rest of the country is enjoying for dinner.

The other popular way that China has of viewing its foods is through the lens of four great cuisines—from the provinces of Shandong, Guangdong, and Sichuan, as well as the city of Suzhou in southeastern Jiangsu Province. This concept probably predates the octet by no more than a few decades at the most. And yet even this idea that there are only four general cuisines has very vague beginnings, for the earliest such mention comes from an early twentieth century literary sketchbook by Xu Ke.[*] But then again, this relatively obscure work merely lumped all of the North together, mentioned the foods of the South and the East in passing, chatted a bit about the spicy tendencies found in Yunnan, Guizhou, Hunan, and Sichuan, and incidentally mentioned the foods of Hubei and Fujian. My studies, though, have shown that all of these allocations are nothing less than arbitrary, for they leave out way more than they embrace.

As far as I was concerned, this meant that nothing here was set in stone, so J. H. and I played devil's advocates with them. We chatted

* *Qīng bài lèi chāo*, or *The Classified Anthology of Qing Anecdotes.*

for a couple of hours over little cups of tea, and pretty soon these elders nodded thoughtfully before declaring that we were probably right, that China had way more than eight cuisines and possibly even more than the thirty-five I managed to list. Nothing could have made me happier, except for the grand meal that followed, when course after course was placed in front of us. Again, few were *málà*, and they all offered thoughtful celebrations of seasonal and exquisitely fresh ingredients.

I AM THE FIRST to admit that I am incredibly lucky, for I managed to tweak my passions into an actual career—writing about the cuisines of China and getting to draw and paint—even though conscious decisions rarely had much to do with how my life unfolded. In fact, I often marvel at how the smallest things ended up having the greatest impact on the course of my life.

If one of my closest friends in high school hadn't been learning Japanese on the weekends, I never would have decided to do likewise. If this new language hadn't hooked me, I never would have gone to the University of Hawaii. If the intermediate Japanese classes hadn't been filled by the time my number was called, I wouldn't have studied beginning Chinese instead. If I hadn't come across that announcement for a year's study abroad, I wouldn't have applied to the programs in Taipei and Tokyo. If some nameless clerk hadn't assigned me to Taiwan, I would have ended up in Japan. If J. H. hadn't worked for that language school, if his wife hadn't insisted that they leave Long Beach and return to Taiwan, if they hadn't decided to split up, if

Mike hadn't thought to invite me to have coffee that one day, if I had found a taxi waiting outside that coffee shop . . . well, any one of those tiny little things would have spun my life into a completely different direction, much like Ray Bradbury's "butterfly effect." But instead, I found love with just the right man, became fluent in Chinese, found myself in job after perfect job, and got the chance to enjoy so many of this ancient country's delectable cuisines at precisely the right place and at exactly the right time.

I'm sometimes asked what the future holds for China's gastronomy, when it will finally be acknowledged as one of the most phenomenal food cultures in the world—up there, at the very least, with those of France and Italy. The thing is, we in the West are only now beginning to understand the treasures that the Chinese table has to offer. Language is, as always, our biggest obstacle, for chefs and restaurants need to be able to communicate a wealth of information to their diners, but often they are stymied before they even open their mouths. And we diners need to step up our game, too. More Westerners need to master Chinese, because only then will we be able to act as cultural conduits and help others to properly appreciate all the wonders this country and these people have to offer.

EPICUREANISM NEVER PROCEEDS in a straight line. Rather, it dips and swerves as history buffets it about. Wars and chaos thrust chefs and kitchens out of the limelight, and then peacetime welcomes them back for feasts and celebrations. Recessions and depressions close restaurants and make even eggs and sugar luxury items, and then, when the good times roll, excess shoves good taste off the table with a sneer as cooks put their personal spin—along with way too much caviar—on what once were time-honored classics. But before too long, when all the dust has settled and good cooks find their way back to the stove, hungry diners arrive and clamor for everything that is good and wholesome and creative.

Artistic geniuses such as Rembrandt, Bada Shanren, and Guo Xi stripped back reality's surface and refracted the truth through paint and ink. Bach, Puccini, and Mozart consorted with exquisite concepts that lay far beyond our mortal world. And it seems to me that the truly gifted chefs of China, Taiwan, and the diaspora can lay claim to artistry on a completely different plane as they commune with ideas that are more than incidentally blissful.

What a wonderful life I've been given, to have had the chance to experience all of this with my ever-hungry husband at my side.

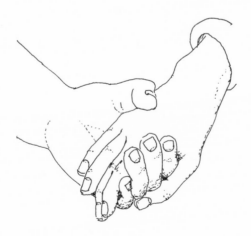

Strange-Flavor Peanuts (V)

GUÀIWÈI HUĀSHĒNG 怪味花生

Just the name alone of this dish makes me happy. *Strange flavor* is a Sichuanese term, and it means that a complex number of seasonings in the dish will fight for your attention. Many versions of these peanuts exist—some with egg whites as the binder, others with different spices—but this is the one we've come to like the best: The toasted nuts are covered with smoked paprika, chiles, Sichuan peppercorns, black pepper, and toasted ground cumin, and the crispy sugar shell is balanced with a nice jolt of salt to keep things on track.

1 pound | 500 g skinless raw peanuts

1 tablespoon smoked paprika

1 tablespoon toasted ground Sichuan peppercorns

1 teaspoon toasted ground cumin

1 teaspoon finely ground dried chiles

1 teaspoon freshly ground black pepper

1 teaspoon fine sea salt

3 tablespoons cornstarch

1 cup | 200 g sugar

¾ cup | 180 ml water

Preheat the oven to 275°F | 135°C. Spread the nuts in a single layer on a baking sheet and slowly toast in the oven about 1½ hours. The edges of your pan will be hotter than the center, so you'll want to stir the nuts occasionally. When the peanuts are fragrant and begin to split down the center, taste one; if the rawness seems to have disappeared, taste a few more from different parts of the pan just to be sure. It doesn't matter whether the nuts are crisp yet; that will happen as they cool. Remove from the oven.

While the peanuts toast, combine the spices, fine sea salt, and cornstarch in a small bowl. Line a large rimmed baking sheet with parchment paper or foil and spray the paper or foil with cooking oil.

When the peanuts are done, combine the sugar and water in a wok and swirl around a few times to ensure that the sugar is moistened all the way through. Bring the sugar water to a boil over medium heat, swirling it now and then rather than stirring it, as the latter would encourage crystals to form. Cover the wok for about a minute so that the steam washes down any crystals on the sides, then raise the heat to medium-high. Swirl the wok now and then (again, don't stir), and as soon as the syrup takes on a golden tinge, but is not yet a caramel, toss in the peanuts all at once. Use a spatula to toss the peanuts in the syrup until they are thoroughly coated. Remove the wok from the heat and rapidly sprinkle the spice mixture over the nuts. Then return the wok to the heat and quickly toss the peanuts to distribute the seasonings evenly.

Remove the wok from the heat and wait about 30 seconds for the sugar coating to start to cool down and harden, then scrape the nuts onto the lined baking sheet. Scoot the nuts around to separate them as much as possible. Cool thoroughly and store in a tightly closed container. *Makes about 3 cups | 500 grams.*

Garlic Lava Pork

SUÀNNÍ BÁIRÒU 蒜泥白肉

One way in which this recipe differs from the traditional methods of preparation is that I add salt and spices to the pork as it simmers in order to both amplify and balance the natural meaty aromas. Be sure to reserve the stock after you cooked the pork; it is delicious. I'd suggest cooking a handful of thinly julienned Asian radishes in it for a great soup (*see* recipe on page 113).

Turn your cucumbers into fine ribbons for this dish. You don't want crunchy distractions, so use a mandoline or a steady hand to make slices so thin you can practically read through them, and they will then offer a very sexy contrast to the cool pork and vibrant sauce. (One of my testers, Michelle, suggests using a vegetable peeler if neither a mandoline or a sharp knife appeals, and that is an excellent idea—stab one end of the cucumber with a fork if you are really anxious about keeping your fingers out of harm's way.)

Note that there is lots and lots of garlic here, but never fear, for it is subtly tamed with an ice-water bath. This secret little maneuver cuts back on the gassiness and stickiness, which in turn allows the garlic's perfume to shine and the individual morsels to glide across the tongue.

1½ pounds | 750 g slightly fatty fresh pork belly or boneless rump
  or shoulder, with or without skin

1 tablespoon whole Sichuan peppercorns

3 whole star anise

1 tablespoon fine sea salt

3 to 4 Persian or other seedless cucumbers

1 green onion, sliced into thin rings, for garnish

½ fresh red chile pepper, sliced into thin rings for garnish
  (optional)

SAUCE

6 cloves garlic, peeled (*see* Tip) and finely chopped

1 to 2 tablespoons sweet soy sauce, or additional regular Chinese
  soy sauce plus sugar to taste

1 tablespoon regular Chinese soy sauce

1 tablespoon oyster sauce

1 tablespoon chile oil (optional)

1 tablespoon balsamic vinegar

1 tablespoon pale rice vinegar

At least 4 hours before you plan to serve it, place the pork in a medium
saucepan and cover with water. Bring the liquid to a full boil, reduce
the heat to a simmer, and blanch the pork, uncovered, for about 10
minutes. Dump out the water and rinse both the pork and the pan.

Return the pork to the pan, cover it with fresh water, and add the
Sichuan peppercorns and star anise. Bring once more to a full boil,

then reduce the heat and simmer the pork for about 20 minutes. Add the fine sea salt and continue to simmer for another 25 minutes, or until the pork can be easily pierced in the thickest part with a chopstick. Cool the pork in the strained stock, and, if you have the time, refrigerate it in the stock overnight.

While the pork is cooling off, prepare the cucumbers: Trim off both ends of each one and use a mandoline, vegetable peeler, or very sharp knife to cut them lengthwise into very thin ribbons. Pile these into a serving bowl or onto a rimmed plate and chill. Cut the green onion and optional chile pepper into thin rings.

About an hour before serving, transfer the pork to a plate. Flick off any clingy peppercorns and star anise and pluck out any hairs you might see at this point. Cut the pork against the grain into very thin slices.

Meanwhile, place the garlic in a small bowl and cover with ice water; this will remove a lot of its stickiness and heat. Set aside. Just before serving, drain the garlic well in a fine strainer and then mix it with the rest of the sauce ingredients, using 1 tablespoon of the sweet (or sweetened) soy sauce to start, then tasting the mix to see whether more is needed.

Fluff up the cucumber ribbons to create an attractive nest. Fan the pork slices across the top. Drizzle the sauce over the pork, but not on the cucumbers, so that the green and white of the cukes remain clean. Scoot the chopped garlic over the pork, then scatter the green onions and optional chile pepper over that. Great with steamed rice. *Serves 4 to 6.*

Tip

Don't use the microwave to help peel the garlic (as described on page 93), for it needs to remain raw in this recipe. Instead, cut off the hard bottoms of each clove before whacking them open with the side of a wide blade. This will make it easy to remove the papery sheaths before you chop up the garlic.

Acknowledgments

A few lucky writers are blessed with a muse, while the rest of us can only hope to land in the capable hands of a phenomenal editor. I fall squarely into the second camp, for Melanie Tortoroli patiently pushed me in the right direction and even plucked the book's title from out of the manuscript. Mo Crist is the invaluable editor who successfully coordinated this book's interior, Ingsu Liu helped me create a great cover, and I was honored to have copyeditors Kathleen Brandes and Judith Sutton work on the final draft. I relied on Beth Steidle, Amy Medeiros, and Becky Homiski for this book's production, as well as publicist Will Scarlett and marketer Meredith McGinnis. And last but certainly not least, my appreciation goes out to the intern who read my proposal and insisted that W. W. Norton publish this memoir: Alegra Padrón. Thank you one and all. You are my dream team.

My endless gratitude to my agent Kimberly Witherspoon. She, along with the incredibly competent Maria Whelan at InkWell Management, matched me up with Norton. My good friend and favorite attorney, Lizbeth Hasse of Creative Industry Law, is another remarkable woman I will always be proud to have in my corner.

Thank you to the official recipe testers who tasted and tweaked and reported back, especially my lovely and talented tester coordinator, Marc Schermerhorn, as well as John Messer, Dirk Van Susteren and Marialisa Calta, Shannon Lyons and Cathy McBride, Michelle Poling, Paul Berrera, and Jenny Hartin.

Of course, I did not tell only my own story here, for this as much about the lives of my friends, coworkers, and family members—mentioned and not, alive and not—as it is about me. Thank you all from the bottom of my heart. And it ought to go without saying that J. H.—my partner in life, love, and dining—deserves the greatest helping of thanks around for always being there for me, for opening all those doors, and for making each one of our years together that much better than the last.

Glossary and Basic Recipes

Bamboo shoots, winter; *dōngsǔn* 冬筍. Edible bamboo shoots have two major varieties: fat winter shoots and thin spring ones. Both have a sweet, vegetal flavor and tender texture when cooked correctly. Winter bamboo shoots hold up to long braises and in soups much better than the delicate spring shoots. Fresh is best, but frozen ones are an excellent substitute. My advice is that you avoid canned bamboo shoots, for they taste of nothing but the can.

Bean curd, firm; *bǎn dòufǔ* 板豆腐 or *lǎo dòufǔ* 老豆腐. Usually sold in sealed plastic tubs with water in the refrigerated section of a grocery store, this is the most common form of bean curd. It is highly perishable, so refrigerate any leftover raw bean curd in a resealable container with fresh water and use it up within a few days. Always smell the bean curd before using and toss it if it smells sour or feels slimy. Also known as doufu, as well as its Japanese name, tofu.

Bean curd, soft; *nèn doufǔ* 嫩豆腐. Sometimes referred to as silken bean curd, this is much more delicate than firm bean curd, has a higher water content, and breaks easily. Unlike firm doufu, which is coagulated with brine, this type is made with refined plaster. Place any unused raw bean curd in a container, cover with water, refrigerate, and use up quickly.

Chile oil; *làyóu* 辣油. Supermarkets tend to carry this, but it's never as good as homemade, so here is a recipe for a deliciously balanced chile oil with a smoky edge. Once you try this, you will never bother with the commercial stuff again. Guaranteed.

  4 whole dried chipotle chiles
  ½ cup | 50 g finely ground dried chiles
  ¼ cup | 25 g coarsely ground dried chiles
  6 large whole dried Thai chiles
  2 cups | 500 ml peanut or vegetable oil
  ¼ cup | 60 ml toasted sesame oil

Tear the chipotles into smallish bits and discard both the seeds and the hard caps. Mix with the other chiles. Combine both oils in a cool wok and add all of the chiles. Bring the oil to a boil before reducing it to low. You only want little bubbles around the edge, as the low heat will allow the chiles to gently season the oil without burning up and turning bitter. Simmer the oil for 25 to 30 minutes, or until the Thai chiles have turned black and the oil is bright red. Remove from the heat and let the oil and chiles sit overnight to blend further. Strain into a bottle and store in the pantry if you use it often, or in the refrigerator, where it will keep for at least a month. *Makes 2¼ cups | 560 ml.*

Chiles, ground; *làjiàofěn* 辣椒粉 or *làjiàomiàn* 辣椒麵. Finely ground chiles have the consistency of ground ginger, while coarsely ground ones look like delicate flakes. The best selection of both fine and coarsely ground chiles can be found in Korean grocery stores with fast turnovers.

Chinese crullers; *youtiao* 油條. Long, tensile, and a bit brittle when toasted, these are China's answer to doughnuts. These are never sweet, though, and the rising agent is baker's ammonia. You can find these in Cantonese delis, where you can buy as many as you like, or in packages of three or four in the freezer section of Chinese groceries. Freeze these if you don't use them right away, and always warm them in the oven to restore their delectable crunch. These sometimes are labeled in English as "long Chinese doughnuts" or something similar.

Chives, garlic; *jiǔcài* 韭菜. Members of the onion family, these taste much like Western chives but are heftier, more vegetal, and, as advertised, taste much more garlicky. Look for bunches that have bouncy, fresh leaves with no signs of decay. To store, remove the rubber band or tie, wrap the bunch in a barely moist paper towel, place in a plastic bag, and refrigerate. The leaves of green onions with a judicious addition of garlic can be used in a pinch as a substitute. Also called Chinese chives.

Cumin, ground toasted; *zīrànfěn* 孜然粉 or *zīrànmiàn* 孜然麵. Toast and grind these as with Sichuan peppercorns (*see* the entry below for Sichuan peppercorns, ground toasted), but no sifting is needed.

Fish sauce; *xiāyóu* 蝦油. Called shrimp oil in Chinese, this is made by fermenting small fish with salt. It is very salty and has a strong fish flavor, but when used in small amounts, it adds considerable depth to savory dishes. Called *nuoc mam* in Vietnamese, the brands I prefer include Three Crabs, Red Boat, and Squid.

Gāoliáng. *See* Sorghum liquor.

Ginger juice; *jiāngjī* 薑汁. To make this, either use an electric juicer or this superbly low-tech method: Set a sieve over a measuring cup, coarsely grate fresh ginger—or pulse finely chopped fresh ginger in a food processor until it is reduced to a paste—and then squeeze out the juice with your fist into the sieve. Make this just before you plan to use it.

Gochujang paste. This thick, red chile paste from Korea has a slightly sweet flavor due to the fermented rice and sugar used in its preparation.

Licorice root; *gāncǎo* 甘草. Called "sweet grass" in Chinese, this refers to the woody root of the licorice plant that is the source of licorice flavoring. In addition to being a common herb in the kitchen, it also has medicinal uses, so you can find it in most herbalist stores, as well as in Chinese groceries.

Longans, dried; *lóngyǎn* 龍眼 or *guìyuán* 桂圓. Called "dragon eyes" in Chinese, these dried tropical fruits are usually sold already pitted. They possess a heady, almost smoky flavor, and can prove addictive. As with all dried fruits, these should feel relatively soft and pliable. Fresher ones tend to be a pale amber color. Get these in Chinese supermarkets and herbalist shops.

Long beans; *jiāngdòu* 豇豆. Most Asian markets carry these in season. The beans should be slender and supple. Look carefully at the stem and tip ends for shrinkage, as this tells you whether the beans have been sitting around for a while and are drying out. Rot indicates, well, rot. Remove the ties or rubber bands, wrap the beans in a damp towel, place in a plastic bag, and refrigerate. String beans are an acceptable substitute for most dishes if you don't plan on wrapping them into wreaths. Also known as asparagus beans, snake beans, and yardlong beans.

Mushroom seasoning; *xiānggū fěn* 香菇粉 or *xiānggū jīng* 香菇精. Made from nothing other than dried mushrooms, salt, and mushroom extract, this MSG substitute is available in bags in most Chinese markets. But it's also really easy to DIY:

1 heaping cup | 20 g sliced dried mushrooms
2 tablespoons | 20 g fine sea salt

Place the mushrooms in a *dry* blender and cover the blender tightly. Blend the dried mushrooms on low speed until they are fine chunks, and then whirl these on high until you have a very fine powder. Keep the cover on the blender for a few minutes to give the powder a chance to settle. Add the salt and pulse the blender a few times to mix. Scrape the mushroom seasoning into a resealable jar and store in the pantry. Do note that homemade mushroom seasoning is slightly saltier and stronger in taste than the commercial stuff, so use accordingly. *Makes ⅔ cup | 40 g.*

Mushrooms, black; *xiānggū* 香菇. This is the favorite Chinese mushroom, bar none. You can always find the dried ones in any Chinese market, but fresh ones are becoming more commonly available. Look for plump caps with natural (not cut) splits across the top. The dried ones taste best if they are soaked overnight in cool water, which also allows their texture to turn both meaty and silky. Don't discard the stems—just dry them out and store them in a covered jar, as they make an excellent mushroom stock. These are similar to the much thinner Japanese shiitake mushrooms, so the latter can be substituted.

Oyster sauce; *háoyóu* 蠔油. The main seasoning in this rich sauce comes from oysters that are fermented in brine. Oyster sauce is savory and salty with a sweet edge. Lee Kum Kee is the original brand and is still the best. Vegetarian versions are also available.

Peanuts; *huāshēng* 花生. Raw peanuts can be found in most Chinese markets and health-food stores. Toasting them is easy:

  1 pound | 500 g raw peanuts

Heat an oven to 275°F | 135°C. Place the peanuts on a rimmed baking pan large enough to hold them in a single layer and slowly roast them for 90 minutes, stirring occasionally. Taste one to ensure no rawness remains, and then cool to room temperature. Store in a closed jar. *1 pound | 500 g.*

Radish, Asian; *luóbo* 蘿蔔. Big, sweet, and juicy, Asian radishes are simply delicious. Listen to Mr. Cong and buy ones that are heavy for their size—with plump rootlets, no bug holes, and a small diameter of leaves. Refrigerate them wrapped in a damp towel inside a plastic bag. Peel the outer layer, as well as any webby underlayer you see. They are delicious raw during the cold months and when superbly fresh. Varieties include Japanese daikon and Korean *mooli*. Their Chinese name is sometimes translated as turnip, but these are definitely another vegetable altogether.

Rice noodles, dry round; *làifěn* 瀨粉 or *mǐfěn* 米粉. Most thicker dried rice noodles will work in the recipe for Yunnan Cold Rice Noodles (page 231), but if you can find the hollow round ones from Jiangxi that look like *bucatini* pasta, you'll enjoy their chewy texture. Available in many Chinese markets.

Rice wine, mild; *mǐjiǔ* 米酒. Also called cooking wine, or *liàojiǔ* 料酒. Mild rice wine is colorless and tastes a bit like Japanese sake. Cooking wine simply has salt added to it. You can use both of these interchangeably as long as you take the salt into consideration. I prefer Taiwan's brands, but see what appeals to you. Be aware that Cantonese rice wine is around 60 proof, which makes it a type of white liquor, rather than a wine, so read the label carefully. Sake or even a dry white wine can be used if mild Chinese rice wine is unavailable.

Rice wine, Shaoxing; *Shàoxīng jiǔ* 紹興酒. A signature flavor of East China and many Chinese *haute cuisines*, this amber brew possesses a wonderful aroma that is a mixture of dried mushrooms and sherry. Shaoxing rice wine is about 30 proof. My favorite brand is Taiwan's TTJ in a square bottle with a red label. More expensive brands are best reserved for sipping. Also spelled Shao-hsing or Shaohsing. Dry sherry is an acceptable substitute.

Sesame oil, toasted; *máyóu* 麻油. When it comes to Chinese cooking, sesame oil is always made from toasted sesame seeds, as this gives the deep amber oil a wonderfully nutty and toasty fragrance. Always check the label to ensure that it is 100 percent sesame oil. The best brands come from Japan, and if you like this ingredient as much as I do, buy it in the economical tins (which usually contain around 56 ounces | 1.6 liters), rather than in small bottles.

Sesame seeds; *zhīmá* 芝麻. As with peanuts, the best raw sesame seeds can be found in Chinese markets and health-food stores. For what it's worth, black sesame tastes the same as white sesame. Toasting them is a snap:

1 pound | 500 g raw sesame seeds

Pour the sesame seeds into a cool wok without any oil, place over medium heat, and toss with a wok spatula until the seeds smell fragrant and start to pop. Taste a few just to make sure. Cool before using. Store in a closed jar. *1 pound | 500 g.*

Shrimp, dried; *kāiyáng* 開洋 or *gānxiāmǐ* 乾蝦米. You can find small bags of these in the refrigerated section of just about any Chinese supermarket or natural-foods store. They should be whole rather than broken, a pale peach color, and pliable. Store these in the refrigerator in a closed bag.

Sichuan peppercorns; *huājiāo* 花椒. Green peppercorns are immature seedpods and the red ones are ripe. In this book, any recipes calling for Sichuan peppercorns refer to the dried red ones. Look for pink husks (not too red, which means they've been dyed, and not too pale, which suggests they're too old) that feel pliable and have a bright, piney scent. You really want just the husks, so discard any shiny black seeds found at the bottom of the bag. Buy these at busy Chinese markets or Chinese herbalist shops. See page 13 for more information.

Sichuan peppercorns, toasted and ground; *huājiāo fěn* 花椒粉 or *huājiāo miàn* 花椒麵. Toasting the Sichuan peppercorns mellows their flavor, and grinding them into a fine powder makes it easy to slip this spice into your dishes or sprinkle it on top of a bowl of noodles. You can buy this ready-made in Chinese grocery stores, but its fragrance and flavor are pale imitations of something you can easily make at home.

¼ cup | 10 g whole Sichuan peppercorns

Place the peppercorns in a dry wok set over medium heat. Stir them almost constantly until the peppercorns begin to pop and gently smoke. Pour the toasted peppercorns into a bowl. When cool, pulverize them in a miniblender or spice grinder. Sift out the hard bits, as this should end up as fine as talcum powder. Store in a closed container, and discard when it loses its oomph. *Makes a few tablespoons.*

Sorghum liquor; *báijiŭ* 白酒 or *báigār* 白乾兒. While the Chinese name is sometimes mistranslated as "white wine," this is actually a clear, high-proof liquor made from grains and pulses, such as sorghum, barley, and dried peas, which is why it's also called "white liquor." Throughout this book, though, sorghum liquor refers in particular to Taiwan's *gāoliáng* 高粱, which is made on the island of Kinmen. Gin, vodka, and most Chinese white liquors are acceptable substitutes.

Soy paste; *jiàngyóugāo* 醬油膏. Popular in Taiwan, this is simply thickened, sweetened soy sauce that's usually used as a dipping sauce or final fillip on a savory dish. Both Taiwanese and artisanal brands tend to be good. Store the artisanal brands in the refrigerator.

Soy sauce, regular Chinese; *jiàngyóu* 醬油. The brands I rely on most come from Taiwan, including Kim Lan and Wan Ja Shan, although excellent organic and artisanal versions are becoming increasingly available. Small-batch artisanal varieties are best kept refrigerated, as they often do not contain preservatives, but commercial brands can be kept in the pantry. Japanese soy sauce and tamari taste very different from Chinese soy sauces, so they are not good substitutes.

Soy sauce, sweet; *tián jiàngyóu* 甜醬油. While regular soy sauce mixed with sugar can be a useful substitute in an emergency, homemade sweet soy sauce is so wonderful that I always use it up within weeks, no matter how much I make. Part of the reason is that this is based on caramel, and the other is that it has a heady mixture of spices and aromatics. Please note that homemade sweet soy sauce is much stronger in flavor and usually saltier than the commercial varieties, so adjust how much you use.

1½ cups | 300 g sugar

¾ cup | 180 ml water, divided

1 (500 ml) bottle regular Chinese soy sauce

1 teaspoon Sichuan peppercorns

3 slices licorice root

2 star anise

1 teaspoon fennel or anise seeds

3 cloves garlic, lightly crushed

6 thin slices ginger

Boiling water, as needed

Place the sugar in a heavy 2-quart | 2-liter saucepan and moisten the sugar with a third of the water. Without stirring, caramelize the sugar over medium high heat. Remove from the heat and wait for a few minutes before pointing the pan away from you and adding the remaining water, which usually will sputter and boil. When the liquid has calmed down, add the remaining ingredients, bring everything to a full boil, and stir to melt the caramel. Watch the pan closely—when a fine foam forms on the surface, keep an eye on it so that it doesn't boil over—and then reduce the liquid until the sauce is thick and syrupy, 20 to 25 minutes. Strain into a measuring cup and add boiling water to bring the sauce to 2¾ cups | 650 ml. Cool, bottle, and refrigerate if you don't use it as liberally as I do. *Makes 2¾ cups | 650 ml.*

It should be noted that Indonesian sweet soy sauce makes a good substitute. The brand I've heard most highly recommended is a Dutch import called Kaki Tiga Ketjap Medja No. 1.

Star anise; *bājiǎo* 八角 or *dàliào* 大料. One of the delightful family of licorice-scented spices used in many of China's cuisines, this is also one of the most beautiful, as it is shaped like an eight-petaled flower.

Sweet-potato starch; *dìguāfěn* 地瓜粉 or *fānshǔfěn* 蕃薯粉. One of my favorite ingredients for coating fried foods. Be sure to check the label to see that it is made 100 percent from sweet potatoes or yams. The best brands seem to come from Taiwan, and the only place to buy it at present is in Chinese supermarkets and online. Cornstarch and tapioca powder are sad substitutes for this unique starch.

Tangerine peel, cured; *chénpí* 陳皮. These are not tangerine peels that you dry yourself. Instead, these dark peels from Guangdong possess a deep perfume that is indescribably delicious. Find them in dry-goods stores and herbalist shops, where short stacks will be tied up with red string into delightful arrangements. Store in a closed container and rinse before using. Also called aged or dried tangerine peel. There is no good substitute, so if you can't find this, simply omit it.

Water chestnuts; *bíqi* 荸薺 or *mǎtí* 馬蹄. These sweet and crunchy corms are like bamboo shoots in that the best are fresh, the peeled frozen ones can be very good, and canned ones should be avoided at all cost. If you are unable to find fresh or frozen ones in your Chinese market, jicama is a great substitute. When fresh ones are available, press them lightly and select only the hardest ones, as softness indicates rot or bruising. Cover fresh water chestnuts with water and refrigerate. If you change the water every couple of days, these little tubers will stay fresh for a couple of weeks.

Winter melon; *dōngguā* 冬瓜. These large, hard-skinned squashes are usually sold in chunks. Look these over for any signs of decay, which includes yellow spots and either soft or translucent areas. Buy ones that are white and firm, that smell sweet and fresh. Use the winter melon up quickly, as it seems to want to dissolve overnight. Smaller, volleyball-size winter melons are showing up in some Chinese markets, and these can be stored like any other hard squash, such as pumpkins.

Yellow croaker; *huángyú* 黃魚. Called "yellow fish" in Chinese because of its lovely golden hue, this round-faced croaker is native to the waters off of East Asia. Once a victim of serious overfishing, the numbers of this wild-caught fish have rebounded so well since the late 1970s that it is no longer threatened. Available fresh, frozen, and dried, this fish is also sold in Chinese and Korean markets as corvina or yellow corvina.

Zhaotong chile paste; *Zhāotōng jiàng* 昭通醬. Named after a city in Yunnan that lies about 250 miles north of Mi'le, Zhaotong-style chile paste is traditional for the Yunnan Cold Rice Noodles on page 231, but unfortunately it is unavailable in the US at this time. The good news is that Korean *gochujang* works in a pinch (*see* entry for *Gochujang*, above), as long as you add ground toasted Sichuan peppercorns and peanuts.

Recipe Index

Subject Index

China:
   Cultural Revolution in, 2, 183,
      250
   ethnicities in, 15*n*, 212; *see
      also specific peoples*
   foot binding practice in, 90,
      182, 219–20
   as one of the oldest civiliza-
      tions, 144
   women and girls not valued
      in, 35, 71*n*, 86, 192, 219–21,
      227–28*n*
   women's rights movement in,
      20*n*, 33, 90
   in World War II, 188–91
   see also North China; South
      China; *specific provinces*
China, Nationalist, 11, 19, 106,
      226
China's cuisines:
   culinary regions, 25–52, 77,
      241, 252–53
   kǒugǎn (mouthfeel) of, 142–45
   magic and wit in, 15, 119–20,
      123–25, 151, 154–55
   pork as central to, 14–16
   principles, 127–28, 144–45
   see also specific provinces
Chinese Civil War (1927–1949),
      11, 19, 21, 143, 179, 188, 225
Chinese language, 58–60
   disconnect between English
      and, 14, 58
   English words adopted by, 59
   history of, 58
   Mandarin dialect, 2, 9, 54

written characters of, 60–61,
      77
Cixi, Dowager Empress, 81
Cong, Mr., 107–10, 113
cumin, 245–46

Dao De Jing, 242
Datun Mountain (Taiwan),
      101–2, 103
David, Elizabeth, 247*n*
Dim Sum Field Guide, The
      (Phillips), 243
Donggang village (Taiwan), 49–52
Donglong Temple (Taiwan), 49

East China, cuisine of, 120–23,
      124–26, 127, 131
Elder Paternal Aunt (*Bómǔ*), *see*
      Zhou Yueming
Elder Paternal Uncle (*Bófù*), *see*
      Huang Longjin
English Bread and Yeast Cookery
      (David), 247*n*

Five Dynasties and Ten
      Kingdoms period (907–79),
      185
foreign concessions, 222
Fujian Province, 184, 186
   cuisine of, 252
Fu Pei-mei, 57, 149
Fuxingyuan restaurant (Taipei),
      120, 122

Gao Zi, 32–33, 36–40, 42
Gobi Desert, 246

Phillips, Carolyn (*continued*)
  lifelong love of food shared by
    J. H. and, 47–48, 50–51, 52,
    56, 103–4, 115–20, 122–30,
    146, 168–69, 240–41, 243–
    46, 249–50
  as Mandarin interpreter, 2,
    138, 238, 239–40
  Mandarin language study of,
    2, 9, 21–22, 54, 61, 77–78,
    253
  mother's relationship with,
    22–23
  at National Museum of
    History (Taipei), 66, 105,
    111, 137, 145
  New Beitou District home of
    J. H. and, 97–101, 153–55,
    159–65
  pig's head prepared and
    cooked by, 153–62,
    165–69
  Shipai District apartment of J.
    H. and, 107, 159
  at University of Hawaii, 1, 14,
    253
  wedding, 210
Point, Fernand, *see Ma*
    Gastronomie
pork, as central to Chinese cui-
    sine, 14–16
Puccini, Giacomo, 255
Pu'er (Yunnan), 215

Qinghai Province, 246
Qīngmíng shànghé tú, 19*n*

Qinling Mountain Range, 246
Qin Shihuang, 17*n*

Radford, Arthur W., 138*n*
Rembrandt, 255
Renee's Garden, 136
rice wine, 58, 116, 120–21

Shaanxi Province, 13, 17
  cuisine of, 17
Shandong Province, 252
Shanghai, 117, 121, 122*n*
Shaoxing (Zhejiang), 120–21
Shénnóng běncǎo jing, 13*n*
Sichuan peppercorns, 13
Sichuan Province, 10, 13, 66,
    147, 189, 191, 237–38, 244
  cuisine of, 252
  dialect of, 53
  street food of, 10, 12–13, 246
Silk Roads, 18
Song dynasty (960–1279),
    227–28*n*
Soochow University (Taipei),
    71–72
South China:
  cuisine of, 78–80, 251
  Guangdong cuisine, *see*
    Guangdong Province, cui-
    sine of
  Hakkas in, *see* Hakka
Southern California, Asian pop-
    ulation in, 73, 78–79
Sui Garden Gastronomy, The
    (*Suíyuán shídan*) (Yuan), 20,
    145–46, 170

Sun-tzu, *see Art of War, The*
Sun Yat-sen, 182
Suzhou (Jiangsu):
    cuisine of, 38, 119, 252

Taipei, 62
    CP's first weeks in, 5–9, 99,
        165
    food establishments in, 21
    high-tech revolution in, 2, 21
    Mandarin language program
        in, 2, 9, 21, 253
    markets in, 7–8, 107–110
    New Beitou District of, 101
    Old Beitou District of, 101–2
    regional Chinese cuisines in,
        2, 17, 19
    Shipai District of, 107, 159
    Songshan District of, 22, 54
Taiwan:
    high-tech revolution in, 2, 21,
        48, 149
    regional Chinese cuisines in,
        2, 17, 19, 47–48
    typhoons in, 12
Taiwan Strait, 11
Tamsui village (Taiwan), 103,
    160
Tang dynasty (618–907), 185
Tang Xuanzong emperor, 66
Teochew, *see* Chaozhou
Tianjin, 81, 84–87, 88*n*, 89, 193,
    212, 216, 218, 222–23, 228
    Japanese invasion of, 222
    Tianjin dialect, 234
typhoons, 12

UNESCO World Heritage Site
    (Yunnan), 224
Ürümqi, 246
Uyghur people, 246

Warlord Era (1916–28), 213
women and girls in China, *see*
    China
World War II, 11, 19, 188
    Japan's surrender in,
        190–91
Wu, Old Lady (CP's Taipei
    neighbor), 154, 162–65

Xi'an (Shaanxi), 17
Xiaozhan, 88*n*
Xinjiang Uyghur Autonomous
    Region, 246
Xu Ke, 252

Yanagi (Liu Yukun's ancestor),
    218
Yang, Chef, 250
Yangtze River, *see* Chang Jiang
Yangtze River Delta, 125, 147
Ye, Mr., 104
Yellow River, 15, 184
Yibin (Sichuan), cuisine of,
    244–45
Yi people, 224, 244
Yuan Mei, *see Sui Garden
    Gastronomy, The*
Yunnan Province, 84, 213, 214–
    16, 231
Yuzhilan restaurant (Chengdu),
    238, 247–250